Cloud's Legacy

The Wild Stallion Returns

Cloud's Legacy

The Wild Stallion Returns

The saga continues in this
companion book
to public television's
NATURE program

by Ginger Kathrens

BOWTIE
PRESS®
IRVINE, CALIFORNIA

For Plenty Coups and the wild horses of the Arrowheads,
who roam in meadows of everlasting green. I will miss you.

Nick Clemente, Special Consultant
Karla Austin, Business Operations Manager
Ruth Strother, Editor
Michelle Martinez, Project Manager
Designed by DeVa Communications based on the original design
by Michele Lanci-Altomare in *Cloud: Wild Stallion of the Rockies*

Additional photographs reproduced with permission: © Trish Kerby, pp. cover, 5, 106, 109; © Mario Benassi, pp. 12, 124, 160; © Brad Edwards Markel—TheNatureSite.com, p. 43; © Linda Crawfis, pp. 94, 100; © Nancy Bjelland, p. 105; © Tony Wengert, pp. 133, 139, 196; © Ann Evans, pp. 153, 158, 162, 174, 197; © Steve Kroshell, back flap.

Library of Congress Cataloging-in-Publication Data
Kathrens, Ginger, 1946-
Cloud's legacy : the wild stallion returns / by Ginger Kathrens.
  p. cm.
Companion book to PBS's second Nature documentary about Cloud, a wild stallion living in the Rockies.
Summary: A filmmaker describes her experiences while making a documentary about a wild stallion in the Rocky Mountains, beginning when Cloud is five years old and starting his own family.
  ISBN 1-931993-12-2 (hard cover : alk. paper)
  1. Cloud (Horse)--Juvenile literature. 2. Wild horses--Rocky
Mountains Region--Biography--Juvenile literature. 3. Kathrens, Ginger,
1946--Juvenile literature. 4. Human-animal relationships--Juvenile
literature. [1. Cloud (Horse) 2. Wild horses--Rocky Mountains Region. 3.
Kathrens, Ginger, 1946- 4. Human-animal relationships.] I. Nature
(Television program) II. Title.

SF360.3.R53K39 2003
599.665'5'0978--dc22
    2003013907

BowTie Press®
A Division of BowTie, Inc.
3 Burroughs
Irvine, California 92618
Printed and bound in Singapore
10 9 8 7 6 5 4 3 2 1

Contents

Introduction

IT WAS A SUNNY MORNING, WARM FOR LATE SPRING ON the remote Arrowhead Mountains of southern Montana. Once the spiritual heart of Crow Indian country, wild horses have wandered this isolated corner of the Rocky Mountains for two hundred years, perhaps longer. I set up my camera on an immense ridge, where miles of meadows were interrupted by deep ravines and dense trees. I filmed a young wild horse stallion who was making unwanted sexual advances toward his father's newly won mare. His father was off playing with bachelor stallions, and the three-year-old was taking advantage of the situation. Then out of the corner of my eye, I saw a flash of white in the forest. Seconds later, a young palomino mare broke out of the trees with her newborn and led him right past my camera. The colt was just hours old and he tottered to keep up with his mother. He was unlike any foal on the Arrowheads for he was nearly white. I had never seen a newborn foal, let alone a wild one. Were they all this fragile, or just this little one? I prayed that he would live.

I have traveled the world filming wildlife, but no wild animal has so completely captivated me as the nearly white wild horse colt I named Cloud. My journey tracking him in his wilderness home is the grandest adventure of my life. Our paths first crossed on May 29, 1995. At the time I thought it was just good luck. Now I believe it was much more than just a chance encounter.

Cloud did live. Within weeks he grew into a strong, remarkably precocious colt. He was the son of the magnificent black stallion Raven, the most powerful stallion on the Arrowhead Mountains. Over the next two years, I watched Raven's forceful son grow into a dynamic bachelor stallion. Footloose and playful, he roamed the deserts, canyons, and high meadows of his remote home with a rowdy group of young stallions.

As a two-year-old, he was captured along with many other bachelors in a government roundup. All the bachelors were sold to the public along with other wild horses. Of the bachelors captured, only Cloud was singled out for release because of his unique coat color. He was given his freedom, but he was alone for the first time. Cloud promptly disappeared, and I searched for him everywhere over that winter. I feared he had died or been stolen.

Back home I was working to gentle the blue roan yearling I had bought after the roundup. He had caught my eye in the wild and when he was selected for sale, I successfully bid on him. I took him home to my ranch in Colorado to live with my two Spanish mustangs. I named the beautiful wild colt Trace. Fearful at first, he came to trust me and we became great friends. Still, I always wished he could have remained wild and free like Cloud.

The following May, Cloud miraculously appeared atop the Arrowheads, stronger and more beautiful than ever. Then in the winter he disappeared, and again I fretted but convinced myself that he would reappear in spring as he had the year before. To my relief he emerged on the mountaintop as a feisty four-year-old. He dared to challenge the husky band stallion, Mateo, for his mares. All summer long he dogged Mateo's band. During the course of many long runs in which he baited Mateo to chase him, Cloud injured his leg and went lame.

A wild horse stallion matures at around six years of age at which time he might start to challenge established band stallions. But Cloud has always been proud and fearless. As a four-year-old, he may have believed he could do anything. Now, I worried that his leg injury might prevent him from ever becoming a band stallion. He went into winter lame and listless. And, he disappeared yet again. This time, I thought he might be gone forever.

But Cloud appeared the next spring as a five-year-old, and he had changed. He was leaner, completely healthy, and determined to start his own family. He fought the elegant blue roan stallion Plenty Coups for his mares. Plenty Coups badly injured his leg during his battles with Cloud and lost his entire band.

Ironically, Cloud did not win a Plenty Coups mare but an older *grulla* female. The mare had given birth to a sickly foal and when her band left, she and her yearling son stayed with the foal. Cloud found them and stood quietly by the mare's side. When the foal died, the mare and her son stayed with Cloud. And so, not in a clash of teeth and hooves but in a moment of stillness, the young stallion achieved his goal of starting his own family. A new chapter in his exciting life had begun. Cloud had become a band stallion.

This is where our story continues.

 *Just moments before, Trace and I had said good-bye to Cloud and wished him and his new family well.*

 **Chapter 1**

Rain Shadow

BRITTLE GRASS CRUNCHED UNDER THE HOOVES OF MY wild horse, Trace, as we crossed a wide meadow atop the Arrowhead Mountains of southern Montana. This was once where native boys came to seek their visions and pray for guidance. It is now Cloud's home. I pressed my legs ever so lightly against Trace's sides and he shifted with ease into a trot. I looked over my shoulder to see the puffs of dust raised by his hooves. *Such an unusually dry season*, I thought. Normally in late August, I could spot a bit of green grass at the forest edges, where the snowdrifts lingered the longest. Not this year. Less than average snowfall over the winter along with little rain during the summer left much of the landscape parched.

Just moments before, I had said good-bye to Cloud and wished him and his new family well. His older *grulla* mare, who was long ago named Queen, was set in her ways—not inclined to follow the lead of a young upstart stallion like Cloud. The mare's red dun yearling son clearly enjoyed the company of a stepfather just a few years older than himself. When Cloud snaked the two, dipping his head low to the ground, laying his ears back, and trotting toward them, the yearling moved obediently along while Queen remained defiant. In time I hoped she would learn to believe in Cloud's ability to protect her and the yearling from ever-present and unexpected dangers.

Trace and I picked up a well-beaten horse trail that would lead us off the top of the mountain. To the right of the trail in a clearing, I saw a familiar black horse and his band. I asked Trace to whoa and pulled out my binoculars. It was the black stallion Raven and his mares. They watched us attentively. Raven is Cloud's father and the magnificent patriarch of the Arrowheads, producing sons and daughters with both the skill and will to survive. "Hello, Raven," I whispered. I will always be grateful to the beautiful stallion and his family for opening up their wild world to me. Even before Cloud was born, each time I came to the mountain it seemed like I could rely on Raven and the mares to appear. For reasons I have often wondered about, Raven found me, rather than me finding him.

Trace and I continued on, climbing to the crest of a high hill at the edge of the immense horse range. From here we could

Queen's red dun yearling son clearly enjoyed the company of his stepfather, Cloud, who was just a few years older than himself.

normally see the Absarokee Mountain Range and Yellowstone. It is less than one hundred miles away and usually visible. Not today. Smoke obscured the horizon and the typically bright blue sky was a hazy gray. It had been like this for several months. The flat-topped Arrowhead Mountains sit in what is known as a rain shadow on the leeward side of higher ranges such as the Beartooth Mountains to the northwest. These high peaks grab the lion's share of both snow and rain, leaving less moisture for the area in the rain shadow. Yet even the Beartooths were dry this year. Within six hours after Trace and I left the mountain, the Forest Service and the Bureau of Land Management jointly closed the entire area. A week later snow blanketed the mountain, burying any threat of fire for the year.

Two weeks after that, I returned to the Arrowheads. The snow had pushed the wild horses down from the top of the mountain onto two huge, windswept ridges called Tillet and Sykes. The twin ridges are separated by a deep, impassable canyon called Big Coulee. From a distance, ravines are densely treed, dark, mysterious places. I once found the cache of a mountain lion in one. The cat had covered the remains of his mule deer kill with sticks, dirt, and leaves. Pieces of deer hide had led me to the spot, which I approached with caution. A bent-over human might look like a four legged prey animal and I certainly did not want to be misidentified. Mountain lions do not normally prey on photographers, and I did

 *Raven is Cloud's father and the magnificent patriarch of the Arrowheads.*

not want to be the first. Their primary prey is mule deer, but they will also kill wild horse foals.

After two days of searching for the horses, I spotted a red horse several miles away near the top of a ridge. Through my binoculars I recognized the blaze marking on his face before he disappeared behind a rock outcrop. It was Queen's red dun son. *Cloud should be nearby with the mare*, I thought excitedly. This was a lucky sighting and I needed to make the most of it. Several hours later I arrived on the ridge, looking and listening. Sometimes you hear horses before you see them—sticks breaking, a hoof striking a downed log, a little snort, or a contented blow as air is expelled out the nose. I sat down to listen.

A chickadee called and was answered by another. A pair of ravens passed overhead. It was so quiet I could hear the wind sweeping through their wings. Then a noise came from the wooded hillside on the slope opposite me. I waited, and in a moment I caught a slight movement. Then Cloud, the mare, and her yearling son wandered into the clearing and crossed to a patch of snow in the shade of a tree. All three appeared healthy. Cloud's coat looked especially beautiful, a shade whiter than it was just a few weeks ago. His thick winter hair was starting to grow in. The horses had yet to spot me and I stayed put, sitting quietly and studying them. They reached down and grabbed bites of snow. Melted snow began to dribble out their noses. Behind the horses a small flock of blue grouse passed through a sunny opening in the forest, plucking grasshoppers off the ground with amazing speed.

I studied Queen closely as the horses started to graze. She looked plump, not nearly as fat as Cloud, but in good shape for her age. She was nearly fifteen—while that's not old for most domestic mares, it is getting up there for a wild one. She had already endured many brutal winters on slim rations. If she were pregnant with

Cloud's foal, I worried the growing fetus would place an added burden on her.

Cloud stopped grazing and yawned. He stood perfectly still, letting his head dip a little as he napped. The sun was warm and the winds light on this sheltered slope. It was the last hoorah of summer. Cold weather was just around the corner.

 *It was the first time I had ever found Cloud*

in winter and I felt like I had won the

lottery.

Chapter 2

Cougar Canyon

Oₙₑ DAY IN LATE DECEMBER, MY FOUR-WHEELER lurched and groaned over the slabs of rock on lower Sykes Ridge Road. Miles farther the road climbs, then drops steeply into Cougar Canyon. I parked at the top of the hill and walked down into the canyon to survey the snow situation. It was only a few inches deep, so I drove down. Sparsely treed canyon walls were pockmarked with caves, which seemed like a perfect place for mountain lion dens.

The road curved next to soaring canyon walls, which throw a perpetual shadow onto the road in winter. The snow was two or three feet deep and wouldn't melt until spring. I started to walk uphill to a view of the open ridges of Sykes, where so many horse bands winter. Two miles out I could see what looked like dun horses. Their golden coats gleamed in the angled light. Their manes

Shaman is one of my favorite stallions, an
experienced dun with a kindly quiet way with
his mares.

and tails were black. *Definitely duns*, I concluded. Two more horses came into view—a black and a *grulla*. Duns and *grullas* have dorsal stripes, leg stripes, sometimes even bold shoulder stripes. These primitive markings are likely holdovers from prehistoric times when the horses were probably even more patterned to camouflage them from predators.

It had to be Shaman's band that I had spotted. Shaman is one of my favorite stallions, an experienced dun with a kindly quiet way with his mares. He had established himself as a band stallion long before I started coming to the Arrowheads. I spotted a few more horses but was disappointed not to find Cloud and his little family.

It was nearly sunset by the time I made it back to the car. Beyond the mouth of the canyon I spotted a *grulla* bachelor to my left, a pretty youngster with a blaze. I suddenly noticed something glowing white far behind him. *Cloud?* I fumbled with my binoculars, hurrying to get them to my eyes before the light failed. I scanned the distant slope and focused on the eerie illumination. *It was Cloud*. The last rays of sunlight reflected off his coat. He looked as though he were lit from within. Without that pop of sun I never would have seen him among the dense juniper trees. I tried to memorize the landmarks around him, the cliff below, and the horizontal line of firs above. *"Tomorrow, boy,"* I affirmed. It was the first time I had ever found Cloud in winter and I felt like I had won the lottery. Now I was determined to get a better look.

The next morning, I headed up the mountain. Just before the Cougar Canyon drop-off, I began hiking up an old mining road between the cliff and the ridge of trees. I spotted Cloud; his mare, Queen; and the yearling. They were foraging on tiny clumps of grass above a shallow canyon. Cloud's coat, so scraped up last summer from fighting, was a perfect soft white now. He looked like a colt again. I will never forget the moment he tottered from the trees with his mother looking so thin and fragile. "Look at you now," I whispered, a little lump rising in my throat. He lifted his perfectly sculpted head and looked across the canyon.

In a few minutes, Cloud and the yearling left Queen grazing on the cliff while they wandered down into the canyon. They climbed the opposite hill onto a half-century-old mining road overgrown with juniper bushes and spiny mountain mahogany. I followed them as they descended into a beautiful valley.

High on a hillside, I noticed Cloud's younger half brother, Red Raven, and he had a mare! The stallion was only four years old. To have a mare at his age is unusual and speaks to the strength and luck of this handsome red roan son of Raven. Cloud gave them a hard stare and the two moved uphill. The mare was a solid blue roan and I recognized her as Blue Sioux. She had been with Plenty Coups when he was injured fighting with Cloud last summer. Plenty Coups lost all his mares and they ended up with a variety of stallions. Cloud's brother took advantage of the situation, picking up the pretty blue roan.

Cloud turned his attention from his brother and Blue Sioux to activity that was going on far down the gently sloping valley. Another horse was coming, a buckskin with a coal-black mane, tail, and legs. "Chino," I said out loud, recognizing him immediately. He was the only buckskin stallion in the Arrowheads. Cloud pranced out to meet him with his neck arched proudly. They touched noses then yanked their heads back screaming in unison. The two stallions spun and kicked. Then they turned back to face each other. Cloud lashed out at Chino with his forelegs in his characteristic two-beat strike, much like a boxer with a lightning fast one-two punch. Snow sprayed as the two spun, shoved each other, and kicked. Just that quickly the ritualistic duel was over. Chino turned and raced back down the valley. Soon he was out of sight.

I left the yearling and Cloud grazing at the base of the hill below Red Raven and Blue Sioux. On my way down the mountain, I could see Queen still high on the cliff. I was surprised that in the past four hours, she had moved less than a hundred yards.

Two months passed before I could return to look for Cloud. I searched Cougar Canyon, where I had last seen Cloud but couldn't find him. I walked into the snowy valley, but there were no horses there. Believing they had moved higher on the mountain, I hiked above the canyon, through deep snowdrifts, and onto the windswept ridges of Sykes. I could see horses. Some were close, perhaps a quarter of a mile away. There was a *grulla*, and on another ridge was Shaman's son, a handsome brown roan bachelor. I saw no other horses—which was a disappointment. It was only three o'clock, but the sun was already low in the west. It would take several hours to reach the car so I left, sliding back down the snowy slopes and slogging through the snow-choked ravines. I decided to start earlier the next morning and hike farther if necessary.

The next day, I walked up through the canyon again. And again I saw the *grulla* on the end of a fingerlike ridge. I was pretty sure it was the same horse I had seen the day before, but this time there were three others with it. One was red—the red dun yearling? I half slid into a wooded ravine and trudged up another slope to get closer. I spotted the yearling again. It *was* the red dun. Had he become a bachelor? There were several young black stallions with him. Then I saw the *grulla*. My heart dropped. It was Queen. When I had seen her alone, I assumed she was a lone stallion or a young bachelor. But the distant figure was Cloud's mare, and the young bachelors were following her. Cloud would never allow that, unless he was injured—or dead! I was convinced he would not have abandoned the mare unless something had happened to him.

 *The two stallions spun and kicked. Then they turned back to face each other.*

 *I half slid into a wooded ravine and trudged up another slope to get closer. I spotted the yearling again. It was the red dun.*

I left to go home to Colorado the next day. Not since Cloud disappeared after the roundup as a two-year-old was I this frightened. *Think positive*, I tried to tell myself. *There has to be another explanation, but what would it be?*

 *Cloud cut diagonally downward across the hill behind the mare and yearling. All three broke into a little trot, anticipating a cool drink.*

Chapter 3

The Search

It WAS LATE MAY BEFORE I COULD NAVIGATE THE treacherous roads all the way to the top of the Arrowheads. Spring had been warm and the water holes would be at least partially thawed. Grass, just starting to green up, would draw the horses to the subalpine meadows like a magnet. As I slowly bumped along the rocky road, I dreaded what I might find. I didn't know if Cloud was alive or dead. I nearly held my breath as I reached the teacup bowl. This is the first big overlook where it is possible to see horses in the high meadows. The bowl is rimmed with cliffs on two sides. On a steep hill on the far side, three mule deer were foraging. They looked up and gracefully melted into the edges of a small stand of pines. Without warning, a flock of ravens flew from the bowl. I walked to the edge of the cliff. Below me was the body of a dismembered horse.

I hiked into the bowl to get a closer look. Bones were scattered but there was still enough hair on the legs to identify the body of a *grulla*. The feet were rather small. The top and bottom jaw of the skull were separated but otherwise intact. A mature male would have canine teeth on the top and bottom jaws, but the skull had none. This might be a mare. Was it Cloud's *grulla* mare, Queen? Bending down I ran my index finger over the teeth. A mare as old as Cloud's would have considerable wear on her teeth and these teeth weren't worn at all. This was not an old animal but a young female, maybe two or three years old. I looked up at the cliff above. She had probably been struck by lightning, standing up there when she was hit, and tumbling off the cliff into the meadow. I left the dismembered skeleton and continued my search for Cloud.

Water holes are good places to look for wild horses, so I headed to the largest one. When I peeked over the hill to the spring-fed water hole, I was not disappointed. Diamond, Cloud's older half brother, along with Cloud's palomino mother and the rest of the family were drinking. The palomino had a foal, a little reddish brown filly. After a normal winter, the hill above the water would be a sea of snow, but this year it was a muddy quagmire. There had been below average snowfall and above average temperatures. A few patches no bigger than a king-size bed were all that remained. I tried to walk on the slick slope and started sliding, so I played it safe and sat down on a rock.

Diamond and the band trailed off toward tall stands of Douglas firs. Suddenly, Diamond stopped. He stared back in my direction. I looked over my shoulder and saw several horses approaching. First was a blue roan mare with a big star on her forehead who was followed by a solid blue roan yearling. Clearly the yearling was the daughter of the mare. The twosome was followed by a third horse who was just cresting the hill. I perked up when I

Cloud and his new mare and yearling

finished drinking and headed north.

saw the top of a light-colored head. It was Cloud! *You're here. You're alive.* He paused to look at me, and I waved as I always did. *It's just me, Cloud. No reason to worry.*

Cloud cut diagonally downward across the hill behind the mare and yearling. All three broke into a little trot, anticipating a cool drink. Cloud looked wonderfully fit; he had already shed his winter coat. About halfway down the embankment, the three tried to slow down but found themselves sliding straight down the hill. They braced on all four legs, finally stopped themselves, then changed direction and walked on a diagonal the opposite way, like skiers traversing a steep slope. The females reached the water and drank as Cloud moved in behind them, skidded into the rear of the mare, and then into the water. What a funny, beautiful horse.

But where did his new family come from? I studied the mare, searching my memory bank. *I know you. Your name is Sitka.* Of course! She had been Shaman's lead mare for years. I tried to imagine how Cloud might have taken her and her daughter from Shaman. I thought back to March. When I found the old *grulla* mare with the bachelors, was Cloud already with Sitka and her daughter? I would bet on it. The old mare may have refused to follow Cloud, so he went up on Sykes without her. Then what? Shaman is no pushover. On the contrary, he is an adept, experienced fighter, and his mares seem to bond with him, appreciating his affectionate, relaxed style. So, how did Cloud outmaneuver him?

What I was beginning to realize more and more was the volatility of wild horse society in the Arrowheads. If a band stallion was not on his toes all the time, he could quite suddenly lose all or part of his family. If this kind of theft could happen to Shaman, it could happen to any of the stallions.

Cloud and his new mare and yearling finished drinking and headed in the direction Diamond had taken, north toward a natural barrier of cliffs that plunge thousands of feet to the Crow Indian Reservation. Cloud's family disappeared into the trees, but I did not follow. Instead, I decided that I must find Queen. If she was alive, she might be carrying Cloud's first foal.

 *Just then, a newborn foal raised its head.*

It was a palomino baby!

Chapter 4

Little Cloud

THE SPRING-FED WATER HOLE IS THE LARGEST, MOST reliable water source on the top of the Arrowhead horse range. Other water holes are at the mercy of snowmelt and rainfall. Of these, the most popular with the horses is a spectacular one in the middle of a subalpine meadow below a rocky precipice. Trees atop these craggy cliffs are favorite places for kestrels to perch. The little falcons launch aerial assaults on unwary birds or unsuspecting grasshoppers from this high roost.

The hillside below the cliffs and above the water hole was a huge snowfield. Slender rivulets tumbled from the bottom edge of the melting snowfield, filling the shallow pond below. The first day of June was hot when I scouted the area looking for Queen. A number of wild horse bands were near. While a more dominant band drank, subordinate groups would wait on the hillside. Other groups cooled off by standing or rolling in the snowfield. Still others grazed in the lush vegetation just below the wall of snow.

I noticed Cloud's younger half brother, Red Raven, coming down the hill with his mare, Blue Sioux, and their new foal. The mare walked into the water and her pale-red foal marched right in with her. I could see the baby was a female, and a self-assured one at that. There was no doubt she was Red Raven's little daughter. She seemed as self-possessed as her father. I knew of no other stallion on the mountain to become a father as a five-year-old. It was quite an accomplishment! When Red Raven and Blue Sioux began to pound the water with their hooves, churning the pond into frothy waves, the foal trotted out, flicking water from the tip of her stubby red tail.

Despite seeing me hiking with camera gear, a group of mule deer bucks ventured onto the snowfield and eventually lay down on the snow. The bucks were suffering from the heat because they had only begun to shed their thick winter coats. I set up the camera and began to film them.

Less than two hundred yards away I saw Plenty Coups coming to water—with two new mares! Both mares had foals. All four had belonged to the old bay stallion, King, who was no doubt too old to compete with the recuperated and determined Plenty Coups. When Plenty Coups injured his leg one year ago, he had lost his family. Now he had stolen an entire band. How quickly the tables can turn. I have always marveled at Plenty Coups, his elegant beauty and his stunning bravery, running on three legs to protect his band. As his new family neared the water, they broke into a lively trot, and the two foals ran and bucked. One was a bright sorrel colt with a big blaze.

Below the hillside of snow, Shaman grazed with his four mares. Near them, I spotted something light-colored in the grass. I

Less then two hundred yards away I saw Plenty Coups coming to water—with two new mares!

couldn't quite tell if it was just a bleached-out rock or something else. The pale yellow shape abruptly moved. *That's no rock.* Just then, a newborn foal raised its head. It was a palomino baby! As it turned to look my way, I saw a huge arrowhead-shaped star on its forehead. On the tip of its nose was a pink snip. That familiar pink spot on the tip of the nose was just like the mark on Raven's nose. It was also identical to the pink snip on the nose of Raven's son Cloud.

Shaman's coal-black mare was grazing just a few feet from the newborn. *This must be the foal's mother,* I reflected, *but what are the chances of a black mother having a pale palomino foal?* In my mind I started to quickly assemble all the obvious clues. There was only one horse who could have fathered this newborn. This must be Cloud's baby! *But how could it be,* I wondered?

The foal—no more than two or three days old—struggled to get up. I could see that it was a male as he walked toward his mother on shaky stiltlike legs. Colts always look gangly, with legs too long for their slender bodies. This colt was not unusual in that regard. But his color was exceptional. There was no other colt on the mountain like this one.

After nursing for a while, he walked a few yards to explore the nearby snowfield and smell the big snowbank. Then he munched a tiny bite. Next, he boldly decided to try walking on the

That familiar pink spot on the tip of the nose was just like the mark on Raven's nose. It was also identical to the pink snip on the nose of Raven's son Cloud.

slushy surface, slipping and sliding and nearly falling down. The danger of falling seemed to excite him as he began to sprint and skate across the icy drift, kicking and spinning, sending sprays of snow flying everywhere, nearly throwing himself off his feet.

As his band moved away, the colt trotted off to follow his mother, disappearing over the hill. Watching the band from less than a hundred yards away were the mule deer bucks who had hastily evacuated the snowfield when the palomino colt began his wild play. Once he was gone, the bucks casually strolled back onto the snow and lay down.

Above the water hole, I caught a glimpse of the palomino colt. He was back, this time all by himself. He stood atop the highest point of the hill, looking down at the bucks. *What shall I name you, you curious little son of Cloud?* I asked myself. *How about Little Cloud?* It wasn't very original, but I was certain it was accurate. He sniffed the air, spun around, and raced off, flicking his little white tuft of a tail.

Later in the day, I found Shaman and his band almost half a mile from the water hole. Besides Little Cloud, the solid black mare had a blue roan yearling with her. *A blue roan,* I thought, *like Plenty Coups. Of course, that's it.* One year ago, Cloud had tried to steal Plenty Coups's band. When Plenty Coups blew out his knee, he ended up losing all his mares, including a black mare with a blue roan foal. Cloud must have bred the mare but been unable to hold onto her when the veteran band stallion Shaman challenged him. That's why Little Cloud and the black mare and her yearling were with Shaman. How ironic, then, that Cloud was able to steal Sitka from Shaman. Little Cloud walked in front of his mother, blocking her way. In colt language this means "Stop, I want to nurse." The mare pushed him aside and took a few more steps before giving in to the colt.

In the meadows, babies born at the height of foaling season began to dance atop the Arrowheads.

I watched as the sun dipped over the hills to the west and the clouds turned from white to orange and red. A band was trailing across the distant rim, silhouetted in the dying light. In the meadows, babies born at the height of foaling season began to dance atop the Arrowheads. Diamond's pair, the *grulla* colt and the older filly, raced in looping circles, celebrating the cool evening.

It was nearly dark by the time I left the colts and made my way back to camp for the night. As usual, I stayed at Penn's Cabin on top of the mountain. The old log cabin, built in the 1920s by Penn Cummings, a local cowboy poet, is as dear to me as a long-time friend—even though I've banged my head on the top of the dwarf-sized door frame dozens of times. I'm sure Penn built a shorter door opening to keep out the cold, but at five feet four inches I still have to remind myself to duck two more inches when entering, or risk unconsciousness.

The next morning I got up early, anxious to find Queen. Cloud, Sitka, and her daughter were in plain sight. Diamond and his family were in the open meadows as well. Plenty Coups was near where I had last seen him the night before, just a few hundred yards from Penn's Cabin. But the youngest member of Plenty Coups's new family was missing. The strong and beautiful sorrel colt had disappeared. I hiked the meadows looking for the sorrel baby. I checked behind Penn's Cabin, along and below the long cliff face,

Little Cloud walked in front of his mother, blocking her way. The mare pushed him aside and took a few more steps before giving in to the colt.

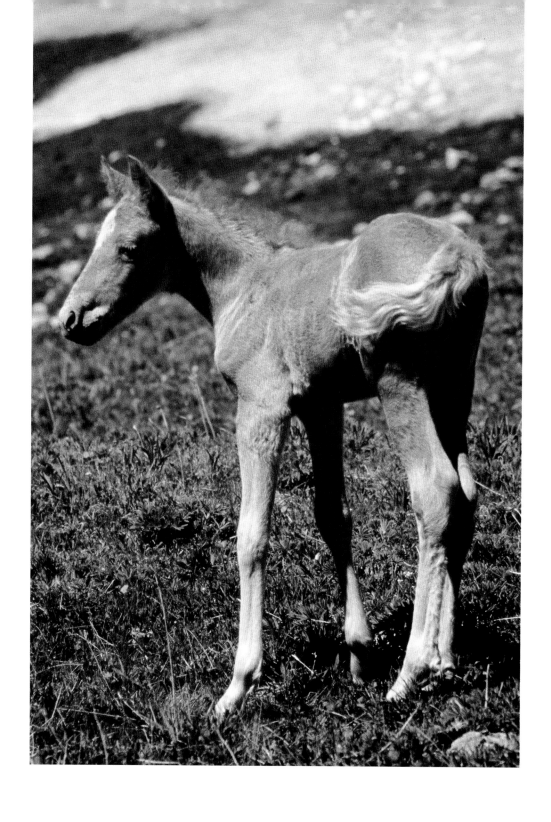

I worried about Cloud's little palomino son. With his pale coat he seemed so vulnerable.

46

bordered by dense forests. *A good hiding place for big cats*, I imagined.

I found no trace of the colt—no tracks, no body, not a drop of blood or one bright orange hair from his beautiful mane or tail. The pretty little sorrel colt was the first of many foals to be killed by mountain lions that summer. A lion needs about one deer every other week to sustain itself. That summer, one foal went missing every ten days or so. Were two lions hunting the range top?

I worried about Cloud's little palomino son. With his pale coat he seemed so vulnerable. At night he would appear like a glow-in-the-dark target to a predator such as a mountain lion.

The sturdy colt was a grulla, soft gray in color with a wide black dorsal stripe; pale leg stripes; distinct shoulder stripes; and big, dark eyes.

Chapter 5

Flint

Ɪɴ ᴇᴀʀʟʏ ᴊᴜʟʏ, Ɪ ᴡᴀᴛᴄʜᴇᴅ ᴀs ᴛʜᴇ ᴡɪʟᴅ ʙᴀʙɪᴇs ᴏғ ᴛʜᴇ Arrowheads investigated their wilderness home. Bighorn sheep lambs were particularly hard to find that year. Perhaps to protect them from coyotes and mountain lions, the ewes kept the lambs hidden just over the lip of the canyon wall, hundreds of feet above the Bighorn River. There, however, they were vulnerable to attack by golden eagles. Any lamb knocked off the canyon wall would feed the eagles' growing chicks.

In the higher forests, spotted mule deer fawns were sticking close to their mothers, watchful of black bears roaming the Arrowheads. The bears will kill newborn fawns if given the chance, just as they will feed on any dead horse they find.

As in years past, a pair of coyotes denned at the edge of the meadow. I got one look at their five tiny pups before the parents discovered me and promptly moved them farther into the limber pine forest. Thinking I might catch a glimpse of them, I sat on the hill in front of Penn's, studying the forest edge beyond the meadow. The edges of any habitat, whether it is a pond or a river or a forest, are good places to spot wildlife. I could see mule deer does in the shadows, carefully lifting one foot then another as they moved from one little sunlit spot to the next to graze. When I saw a dark horse moving through the trees, I went to investigate.

I discovered Sitka's yearling daughter in a clearing with Cloud. There was no mistaking his bright coat. I got closer and found Sitka as well, and standing somewhat apart on a gentle rise, her newborn foal! The sturdy colt was a *grulla*, soft gray in color with a wide black dorsal stripe; pale leg stripes; distinct shoulder stripes; and big, dark eyes. *Oh, how lovely*, I thought. It was difficult to tell that his mother had just foaled. Wild horse mares are amazingly resilient and strong. Sitka had given birth many times and was a caring mother. But I wondered how Cloud was dealing with a baby. This would be his first colt to watch over and protect.

The little colt was watching the deer in the forest and whinnied at them as if he thought they might come out to play. When his mother approached, he dutifully followed. Sitka walked to Cloud, and the colt, instead of avoiding the big stallion, walked right up to him. Without hesitation, the little foal reached up to touch Cloud's nose. But he was too short. Cloud gently dropped his head and sniffed. *Oh, Cloud*, I said to myself, reacting to the stallion's protective and loving gesture. The two touched noses for a few more seconds, and the colt walked on. The baby was Shaman's son by blood. I could see that stallion in him—the sturdy build and the bold, primitive-looking stripes on his shoulders. In every other way, though, this colt was Cloud's son. Their relationship was one I marveled at in the months to come.

The colt stopped to stare at the mule deer does. *You should have a name*, I told myself. Beneath my feet were bits of red, brown, and gray rock. The Arrowheads were named for the rocks so abundant here, hard rocks from which the Crow Indians fashioned their arrow and spear points. *Flint*, I decided, *I'll call you Flint*. At the time I had no idea that Flint would one day need every bit of toughness his name implied.

The colt investigated the limber pines at the forest edge before bending his legs with some difficulty and dropping to the ground. Within seconds, he laid his head on a cushion of pine needles. Broken sunlight filtered through the pine boughs as chipping sparrows twilled a cheerful little song and flitted amongst the low growth around the sleeping colt.

Cloud nickered to Sitka, who stood a few yards from her sleeping foal. The stallion approached her from the rear, gently sniffing. She responded by kicking him in the chest and walking closer to Flint. Cloud could smell that the mare was coming into heat, but he got the message that she was not yet willing to breed.

That afternoon, I finally located Cloud's *grulla* mare, Queen. Near Penn's Cabin, fir trees grow in dense clusters. Several hundred yards away, I noticed movement in those trees and went to check it out. The old mare was standing in the trees with a bachelor stallion. She moved a bit, giving me a better angle, and I saw that she looked thin—unlike most of the mares, who were fattening up by July. Her hipbones protruded and I could see her backbone. As horses get old, they start to lose muscle mass and look bonier. I didn't know if her condition was just the natural aging process at work or whether the mare wasn't well. If she was pregnant, I couldn't tell. I hoped not, considering her appearance.

A few days later, Cloud and his little family moved into the teacup bowl. His father, Raven, grazed just a hundred yards

Cloud could smell that the mare was coming into heat, but he also got the message that she was not yet willing to breed.

 *A few days later, Cloud and his little family*

moved into the teacup bowl.

away with his band. Plenty Coups and his new family were nearby and in the back of the bowl, bachelors dashed through trees, rearing and biting at each other's legs. I could see Shaman on the far hill with Little Cloud and the rest of his band. But Cloud paid no attention to any of this for he was focused on his mare, Sitka. He trotted up to her, speaking in soft snuffling tones as he touched her face and rubbed his nose on her flank. She responded by shrieking and striking him in the chest with a hoof. Rather than moving away, however, she backed into Cloud and they bred. It was mid-July. Nearly a year from now she might give birth to Cloud's very own foal.

 *Cloud looked up to see the bachelors above and below. He seemed to sense this could be trouble.*

Chapter 6

The Bachelors

Flint watched Cloud and his mother breed. As if imitating Cloud, he marched up to his yearling sister who slept in the bowl. Flint began nibbling on her ears, pawing her back, and being a general nuisance. The filly laid her ears back, but that didn't deter the persistent baby. To get away from him, the yearling filly got up and walked to her mother with Flint hanging onto her mane.

With his little family of three safely grouped together, Cloud took the opportunity to visit a stud pile some one hundred feet away. He walked over and leaned down, putting his nose on the mound of stallion nuggets. Then he inhaled. A horse learns a lot about his world from smell, and communal stud piles are major communication hubs. Cloud could tell which males had defecated there and how long ago, and he could probably tell the health of the depositors. After he finished receiving messages, he turned and left

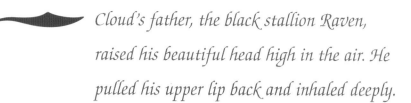 *Cloud's father, the black stallion Raven,*
raised his beautiful head high in the air. He
pulled his upper lip back and inhaled deeply.

a message of his own, signaling his claim to the area and informing one and all that he is a potent stallion.

Cloud's father, the black stallion Raven, raised his beautiful head high in the air. His long forelock separated, falling on either side of the white star on his forehead. He pulled his upper lip back to expose his teeth and inhaled deeply. Raven smelled the sweet aroma of Sitka and turned to stare at his son's mare.

As Cloud headed back to his band, Raven left his. He made his way through the sagebrush toward Sitka. Cloud quickly walked out to intercept his father, standing nose to nose with the black stallion. What an extraordinary pair, two respectful warriors sizing each other up. Until very recently, Raven was the most dominant stallion on the Arrowheads. Three of his sons, including Cloud, are young band stallions, and three of his daughters are reproducing mares. The magnificent black stallion is not a youngster anymore, but he is still a force to be reckoned with. Suddenly the two screamed, whipped their heads apart, and reared up. Then they walked away as if absolutely nothing had happened.

Meanwhile, Flint had walked to a gentle slope where he began to dig little holes in the ground with his tiny hooves. Once he had succeeded in clearing a small piece of earth, he licked it. Did he like the taste? Wild horses dig for their own salt and minerals, which we must put out for our domestic horses. But how did this little fellow know what to do at only a few days old? Maybe he watched his mother or Cloud or his older sister. Young horses learn quickly by observation and Flint promised to be a fast learner.

During the course of the day I kept watching Shaman's band, waiting for Little Cloud to do something that I might film. But the colt stood quietly behind his mother or lay in the sun on the hillside. By the late afternoon, I realized I had not seen him nurse. When he did get up, he walked to his mother and swallowed with

some difficulty. Then he lay back down. I hoped the colt was all right.

At sunset, Cloud and the band wandered out of the bowl in the direction of the snow-fed water hole. The sun peeked out from threatening storm clouds and dipped behind the hills to the west. Instantly, the vibrant green meadows dimmed to a muted gray while the distant desert, still in sunlight, was flooded with pink light. I could hear the faraway rumble of thunder.

Sitka led the band to the snow-fed water hole. Cloud waded into the deepest part and lay down. He rolled back and forth making waves then got up to paw. This was the first time I really had seen Cloud relax and just enjoy the water. Flint watched but did not venture in, much like Cloud when he was a foal. After Sitka drank and pawed a bit, she, Flint, and the yearling climbed the rocky hill above the pond. The mare stood motionless while her son nursed.

It is the role of the lead mare to guide her band, and Sitka was confident and experienced. She knew the best grazing spots, where to find water, and when and where to escape the wrath of a violent storm. Cloud seemed to respect the mare. He had followed Sitka up the hill, where he rolled and started to graze.

I don't think he noticed bachelors moving in all around him. Four roamed the hillside above and another four were coming uphill from the water hole. Cloud looked up to see the bachelors

 *During the course of the day I kept watch-ing Shaman's band, waiting for Little Cloud to do something that I might film.*

above and below. He seemed to sense this could be trouble. The bachelors stopped playing now and again to look over at Cloud. It was Sitka they were after and Cloud knew it.

One-on-one these young bachelors weren't a serious threat to Cloud's family. But working together they could split the little band and cut the mare out. In the melee, Flint could be injured or killed. Once when Cloud was barely two weeks old, I had watched as two bachelors worked together to steal Raven's entire band. Raven was off cavorting with bachelors when two stallions swept in and drove the band away—mares kicking and foals desperately trying to keep up with their terrified mothers. When Raven returned, he followed the thieves and won the band back in short order, but it was a tense moment. I wondered if Cloud remembered the panic of that day six years before. I believed he did.

Before the bachelors got within a hundred yards, Cloud made his move. Like a rocket, he shot toward the four who took the high ground and ran them over the hill. Then he galloped back to engage the four who ran below. Cloud raced across the hill as lightning flashed in the distant valley. The four immediately turned tail and ran with Cloud on their heels. The thunder rumbled as Cloud galloped across the water hole dam, his ears flattened menacingly against his head. He sent the bachelors into full retreat. Not one of the eight would stand and fight.

Then Cloud dashed back up the hill to his family. He gave the bachelors one last look and calmly started to graze. The whole time, Flint had stood with his mother, watching and learning. Then the little *grulla* broke into a gallop of his own, racing in circles and kicking up his heels. He stopped, sniffed the air, whinnied, and ran some more. The light faded in the desert, yet Flint continued to celebrate as a cool breeze whipped across the summer meadows of his home. He ran up to his stepfather and nibbled his mane. Cloud stopped grazing and patiently turned to the colt, giving him a reassuring nuzzle. Exhausted, Flint collapsed in a heap beside his family. As the thunder faded away, I imagined I could hear the colt sigh with contentment.

 *During one July afternoon, distant thunder rolled and wild horses began trailing into the teacup bowl.*

Chapter 7

Danger on the Mountain

WEATHER IN THE ARROWHEADS CAN BE AS WILD as the landscape. Flint was just a little over a week old when potentially dangerous weather patterns began developing. Dark thunderclouds would often build in the west, and with little warning they would rush across the sky, turning a warm day unpleasantly chilly.

During one July afternoon, distant thunder rolled and wild horses began trailing into the teacup bowl. Band after band arrived: Shaman and his family, including Little Cloud; Cloud's band; Raven's family; Cloud's brother Diamond, his palomino mother, and their band; and Plenty Coups's band along with many others. Never before or since have I seen so many Arrowhead horses concentrated on the mountaintop. From my view at the edge of the cliffs, I counted over seventy horses.

 *In time, the storm passed and the horses*

moved back into the open.

By mid-afternoon the sky blackened and gusts of wind whipped the limber pines. Suddenly, a bolt of lightning struck the cliffs less than a hundred yards to my right. Simultaneously, a deafening clap of thunder echoed over the mountain. The horses nearest the cliff wheeled instantly and raced in the opposite direction. Like a chain reaction, the bowl erupted with stampeding horses. As the thunder cracked, one bolt of lightning after another flashed. It was as if someone were flipping a light on and off in a darkened room. Then the rain started to fall, sleetlike at first, followed by big drops wind driven into slashing sheets. Cloud ran far upslope and stood near a solitary limber pine with his butt to the driving rain. Sitka, the yearling, and Flint, huddled together behind three small trees. They, too, turned their rear ends into the wind and rain. Some horses ran away completely, galloping over the hill toward the big snow-fed water hole.

Through the rain, I spotted Shaman's band. His mares had wisely led the group to lower ground at the back of the bowl in the thick forest. I could see Little Cloud in the trees with his mother and believed he was safe. In time, the storm passed and the horses moved back into the open. The temperature had dropped thirty degrees and the foals loved it. One little blue roan filly ran in circles, bucking. Then she stopped and reared and stood on her hind legs, turning in a circle like a ballerina. Flint watched and did a little jig of his own that ended in a kick at his yearling sister. I will always wonder why the horses came to the bowl that day as the storm brewed. It is a place where at least four horses had been struck and killed by lightning in just the past two years. Surely they knew something I didn't.

The next morning dawned cloudless and warm. The horses had spread out once again. Shaman and Cloud, however, were back in the bowl along with Plenty Coups's family and Raven and his band. Flint ran in circles and jumped sagebrush. He glanced over at Plenty Coups's pretty little *grulla* foal. I knew he wanted to play with her, but Flint was an obedient colt. He loved to have fun but he also stayed close to his family and paid attention to the subtle cues of his parents. When Cloud laid back his ears even a little and started to lower his head, Flint quickly picked up the message, moving in the desired direction. If Sitka wanted him to get up or move or come closer, he read her body language and did whatever she wanted. Were he a human boy, I imagine he would have been the track team star who dutifully completed all his homework and brought home straight A's.

Unlike Flint, Little Cloud lay on the far hill and slept. Over the past few weeks, his pale palomino color had faded to near white, like his natural father's. But his personality seemed to be fading as well. The once curious little colt, so similar in character to his father, Cloud, was disappearing before my eyes. I believed he was sick.

Death camas, a deceptively delicate wildflower, was blooming in profusion in the high meadows. Before the flowers open, the slender stems look like clusters of tempting tall grass. Did the colt sample the poisonous plants? Just a pound of any part of the flowers can kill a sheep. *How much would a colt need to eat to make him sick?* I worried. *Even worse, how much would kill him?*

When Cloud laid back his ears even a little and started to lower his head, Flint quickly picked up the message, moving in the desired direction.

When Little Cloud finally did get up, his mother came to him as if encouraging him to nurse. But he just stood beside her. The band moved up the hill, grazing. Little Cloud took a few slow steps and stopped as if the effort tired him out. As his family disappeared over the hill, his mother whinnied for him. If he heard her, he didn't answer. Instead, he listlessly walked to a tall fir tree and lay down beside the trunk. He stayed there for hours. Late in the afternoon, I caught a glimpse of his band again on the very top of the hill. His stepfather, Shaman, started down toward Little Cloud. As he got close, Shaman laid his ears back. *Get a move on*, seemed to be the message. The colt got up and ever so slowly put one foot in front of the other, climbing the slope. He inched past Shaman, and the stallion fell in right behind the colt. The two slowly disappeared over the hill.

That evening I looked for the band, but I couldn't see Shaman's family anywhere in any of the open meadows. The next day I walked into the forest below the teacup bowl—to the snow-fed water hole and down the steep slopes leading to Big Coulee. I found a few horse tracks but none from a foal. The wooded hillside was peppered with bear scat. Sego lilies were scattered in the bright clearings, their delicate off-white petals reaching upward to the sun. I walked into the deeper forest through thick cobwebs draped across old game trails. It was a dark and forbidding place. *Where have Shaman's mares taken the band?* The cheerful call of a yellow-rumped warbler brightened my spirits, and I realized the forest seemed forbidding only because of my worry. Hours later I came out below Penn's Cabin. The next morning, I returned home to Colorado without knowing the fate of Little Cloud. I feared Cloud's son was dying.

In August, when I returned, horses were even more difficult to locate. The open meadows were drying up and it was hot.

Little Cloud took a few slow steps and stopped as if the effort tired him out.

So the bands started to graze on the green edges of forest groves, then they would step into the shade of the trees to nap. In previous years, I have walked within a few yards of bands of horses, passed right by without noticing a one. If a horse hadn't shaken his head, I would have missed the band the second time I passed, too. *Imagine how easy it would be to nearly step on a motionless mountain lion*, I thought at the time.

I walked down a hill where I'd seen Shaman in years past, a sheltered little valley broken by dozens of tree clusters—some the size of a small house, others as big as a football field. I circled each cluster and finally saw Shaman's band emerging in single file from a stand of firs. First the dun mare walked out followed by her dun daughter, then Cedar, the lovely young *grulla* daughter of Raven and Grumpy Grulla emerged. Attached like Velcro to Cedar's shoulder was a stout bay colt with a tan nose. He was only a few days old. Then I saw Shaman and the black mare. My heart sank. Where was Little Cloud? I walked around to get a better look at the path they had taken, and in the dark recesses of the forest, I saw movement. It was Little Cloud! He walked slowly out looking fine physically. In fact he had grown taller. I watched him nurse and nibble around on tall tufts of grass. He watched the newborn colt but, strangely, made no effort to play with him. And he had ample opportunity, for this foal had energy to burn. The rambunctious colt dashed in and out of the trees, leapt over a log, circled the entire band, and then repeated the same looping course over and over again.

Even the presence of this high-energy baby failed to enliven the once vibrant spirit of Little Cloud. *What had happened to the little foal I watched sprint in the snow only a few months before? Would he ever come back?* I wondered sadly. The newborn continued to race about, getting so out of control that his mother, Cedar, ran behind him, perhaps fearful he would just keep running and she might never see him again. *What a good young mother*, I thought. Her son was strong and full of life. She was healthy and I could see that she had a lot of milk. The colt's father, Shaman, had successfully raised sons and daughters for nearly a decade. Yet within two weeks, Cedar and Shaman's colt was dead, killed by a mountain lion. Ironically, Little Cloud lived.

 *Right from the first time I saw the newborn,*

I tried hard not to fall in love with her.

Chapter 8

Cloud's Filly

ANOTHER FOAL WAS BORN IN THE FIRST PART OF August when the high meadows were losing their green luster, fading into shades of gold and brown. Queen, Cloud's first mare, foaled. From the time I first saw her in early July, she had not regained the weight she had lost over the winter. Having a foal seemed out of question, at least I had hoped so. The mare had rejoined her former band stallion, King, and the two were together when the little filly was born.

Right from the first time I saw the newborn, I tried hard not to fall in love with her. And to protect myself, I refused to give her a name for I knew her survival was going to be an uphill fight. She was small and thin and her coat was a dull grayish brown with a narrow little dorsal stripe. Her legs were like toothpicks compared to the other Arrowhead foals. Her mother didn't look much better.

 *Over thirty foals were born. Only twenty survived to see the end of summer.*

The old mare's hipbones and backbone protruded out of a once strong frame. She probably wasn't producing much milk, which the foal needed to overcome her poor condition. Yet the tiny filly was Cloud's daughter, and I hoped beyond reason that the inherited strength of the Raven line would somehow pull her through.

The old band stallion King was in poor shape, too, with ribs showing under his once lustrous mahogany bay coat. The stallion, mare, and foal were a ragtag trio, a truly sorry sight to behold. The filly seemed to be working hard just to keep up with her mother, as if walking were a struggle. Yet one cool summer evening, when sunlight angled across the meadows painting the landscape gold, I saw her dance. She suddenly kicked up her tiny heels and sprinted past King and Queen. Right then I wondered *What if she had been born to a younger, healthier mother?*

Cloud's filly was one of the last to be born that summer, the summer I call the year of the cat. Over thirty foals were born. Only twenty survived to see the end of summer. I caught a glimpse of a mountain lion only once. I never saw the big predators attack. Still, I knew that they were around, silently waiting, invisible as they lay frozen in the shadows of the trees and deadfall. *Surely Cloud's little filly would eventually fall prey to the big cats.*

 *Knowing Plenty Coups, I was convinced he*

would have fought like a tiger, even if injured.

Chapter 9

Saying Good-Bye

THE NEXT DAY, IN THE LARGEST OF THE OPEN meadows I was surprised to see Cloud in the midst of agitated horses. The band stallion Star was making a run at him, and Cloud retaliated by rushing toward Star, rearing, striking out, and running him off. Then Cloud swiveled, his neck arched regally, and he flew toward another young band stallion named Morning Star. Just before he got to Morning Star, he stopped and stomped his foot on the ground, emphatically warning the stallion to stay back. Then Cloud did an about-face and rushed back to his band, a band that had grown larger in the past twenty-four hours.

Besides Sitka, her yearling, and Flint, there was a new bay yearling filly—and a blue roan mare with her yearling daughter. I recognized the mare and her daughter. They had been with Morning Star since spring. When I looked over at Morning Star, I realized he was with Plenty Coups's two mares and the foal. *What had happened? Had Morning Star stolen Plenty Coups's band?* Morning Star's dark bay coat had a few little scrapes, but he wasn't bloody or scarred as if he had been fighting. Knowing Plenty Coups, I was convinced he would have fought like a tiger, even if injured.

I pieced together clues to explain what might have happened. Morning Star couldn't keep both the blue roans and Plenty Coups's *grullas* together. If mares don't like each other and refuse to accept each other as part of one family, it is only a matter of time before the band structure shatters under the weight of constant conflict. Cloud must have taken advantage of the situation and stolen the blue roans.

I realized also that Cloud faced the same situation. He had a window of time to forge a family out of two factions or lose them to a challenger. That's why Star was hanging around. He sensed that the band was not unified and stealing a mare or two might be possible.

When I noticed vultures circling in and out of the treetops far beyond the meadow, where I have so often seen bears, I left Cloud and went to investigate. I approached the side slope of a narrow valley through the trees, not knowing what I might find. I saw the gray lump on the hillside and within seconds the small black bear who was feeding on it. The bear pulled on the legs of the

Cloud must have taken advantage of the situation and stolen the blue roans.

grulla horse and rolled it down the hill. Then the bear raced into the trees. I lifted my binoculars and studied the body. "Konik," I whispered sadly. The old band stallion Konik was dead. I believed it wasn't lightning this time.

Before I started coming to the Arrowheads, Konik had the largest band on the mountain. But in recent years he had lost all his mares. When Konik stopped trying to win them back, he seemed to lose heart. During the last few weeks he had been acting sick, even though he still looked fine. He refused to join the young bachelors and he rarely associated with another exiled leader, the former band stallion Blackie. I don't believe Konik could come to grips with his diminished status. In the end he gave up, lay down, and died.

The little black bear came back out of the trees and sat down next to Konik to feast. At least four different bears came to feed on the protein-rich carrion. After the little black bear left, a bigger bear with a rich, deep brown coat sat and ate. Even the beautiful cinnamon bear I'd seen several times before came to the banquet. The bears rolled Konik's body around. One sure way to tell if bears have been eating on a carcass—they always roll the body, twisting it into contorted, grotesque positions to access its meatiest parts. Even in death, Konik was valuable.

I returned to follow Cloud and watched as he drove his new band uphill. The mares seemed to move along together without biting or kicking each other. That was a good sign. He was pushing them toward the crest of the long ridge when I became distracted by something sticking up in the air, looking like a limb on a dead tree. As I went higher, I realized I was not looking at a dead tree limb but at a horse leg. My stomach knotted. The leg, pointing into a clear, deep blue sky, was black. It was attached to a blue roan. The mystery of how Morning Star acquired Plenty Coups's family was suddenly and sadly solved.

Before I started coming to the Arrowheads,
Konik had the largest band on the
mountain.

Plenty Coups lay dead on the ridgeline, no doubt a victim of one of the vicious lightning storms that had ripped over the Arrowheads in recent days. It is always difficult to find a dead horse, but it was especially difficult to find this one. Gallant Plenty Coups, dead—it seemed impossible.

Over the next few weeks and months I visited his body often. I was unable to let go of the stallion who seemed to fulfill the legacy of his namesake, the great Crow Indian Chief Plenty Coups. The parallels between the horse and his human counterpart have always fascinated me. The man, Plenty Coups, bridged the period when the Crow hunted buffalo and successfully defended its land from raiding Lakota and Blackfeet tribes through the settlement of the West by whites. He was a chief during the difficult time when native people became prisoners on reservations. When he was a boy in the 1850s, long before the white man threatened his lands, Plenty Coups had a vision warning him that fighting the white people would be fruitless and could cost the Crow Indians their homeland. He wisely helped negotiate his people's right to remain in Montana on the land they loved. Under his guidance, a reservation was carved out of a fragment of the best of the original Crow lands. The great Chief had no children. Rather, he adopted orphans and raised them as his own. He died in 1932 near the base of his beloved Arrowhead Mountains.

In 1994, when I first started coming to the Arrowheads, I heard a story about a young blue roan stallion named for the great Chief. It was rumored that the bachelor stallion was roaming the mountaintop with a male foal. Most people thought the story a ridiculous one, but I saw the stallion, the foal, and the foal's severely injured *grulla* mother. The mare must have broken her hip and could barely walk. When the mare could go no farther, Plenty Coups allowed her son to travel with him. Like the Chief, Plenty Coups had adopted an orphan.

In 1994, when I first started coming
to the Arrowheads, I heard a story
about a young blue roan stallion
named for the great Chief.

 *The bears never touched the body of*

Plenty Coups.

That same fall there was a roundup, and some mares and foals were separated in the mad dash down the mountain. The cowboy wranglers were careless and left foals behind when they drove their mothers into corrals nearly twenty miles below. So Plenty Coups added more orphan foals to his band. They were his first family.

Some things are unexplainable, and that was the case with the gallant stallion Plenty Coups. When I visited his body, I wondered why it lay undisturbed. I imagined the stallion was really alive and simply taking a nap atop the ridge. Yet over time, the carcass dried up, leaving a perfect mummified corpse. The stallion's dark eyes, once gleaming with intelligence and power, were hollow sockets now. Locked in his steady gaze was the teacup bowl, the long lizardlike form of Sykes Ridge where he had grown up, and the Bighorn Mountains beyond.

The bears never touched the body of Plenty Coups.

 *It was on the path to the vision quests that
I found Cloud and his band.*

Chapter 10

Cloud's
Growing Family

IN LATE AUGUST, IT WAS STILL DRY. WEEKS LATER IT WAS drier still. Most of the West was in the throes of a continuing drought. Storms blew through, full of dangerous dry lightning but little rain. The wild horses responded to the dry conditions by moving into the highest meadows of the Arrowheads.

One morning I left Penn's Cabin early, hiking in and around the forests near the spring-fed water hole. One little sheltered glade after another opened up in the fir forests. The trail led to the cliffs overlooking the vast Crow Reservation. Historic vision-quest sites on the edge of the rampartlike precipice still mark the spots where Indian boys fasted for days, waiting for spiritual enlightenment. Sometimes they were lucky and a vision would be revealed of an animal who would guide and protect them.

Small water holes near Penn's Cabin had a few inches of red, muddy liquid. That's where I spotted Queen, King, and Cloud's little filly.

It was on the path to the vision quests that I found Cloud and his band. There was the new mare, her yearling daughter, and the bay yearling, plus Sitka, Flint, and Sitka's daughter. I watched for any of the acrimony so typical when a new mare is brought in with an older, well-established one. Sitka didn't seem to mind the other blue roan mare. They weren't chummy enough to mutually groom each other, but neither mare laid back her ears or bit at the other, as I've seen before in such situations.

Flint took a particular liking to the bay yearling filly. He pestered her in the same way he nagged his own sister. He jumped on her back, wrapped a front leg over her neck, and nibbled on her mane. The filly only wanted to be next to Cloud. She and the stallion groomed each other often, and Flint loved to horn in. While Cloud groomed the filly, Flint groomed Cloud. Stretching up his square little head, he could barely reach his stepfather's jaw, grabbing and gnawing on the stallion's face. After a few minutes of this, Cloud stopped scratching the filly's neck and walked away with Flint still jumping for his face. I never saw Cloud discipline Flint for this or be cross with the colt in any way.

In early September, snow had fallen and mostly melted by the time I arrived back on the mountain. The open meadows were completely dried up, but the ponds now had a bit of water. Small water holes near Penn's Cabin had a few inches of red, muddy liquid. That's where I spotted Queen, King, and Cloud's little filly. All three looked thin.

Cloud's band was nearby and Flint, for no reason that I could see, started running big circles around his band. He seemed so full of himself that he just couldn't stand still. As he ran past Cloud, the stallion and the bay yearling leapt into the air and bucked. Flint was the catalyst for the band. They all broke loose in a spontaneous dash across the dry meadows. At that moment they looked like carefree youngsters again. I turned back to see the little filly watching Cloud's family. How I wished she had the strength to run, just for the fun of it, like Flint. But wishing wouldn't make it happen.

Shortly after sunset, Cloud and the band trailed out on the hill beyond the spring-fed water hole. All seven stood looking toward the colorful western sky. Beyond them, the Beartooth Mountains zigzagged across the horizon. A coyote called, his voice echoing away, unanswered. Cloud didn't seem to notice. He stood motionless, watching the clouds turn from orange to deep red and finally to gray. Within days, his world would be turned upside down.

Wild horses were suddenly pushed off the meadows on a run that would end twenty miles farther at the base of the mountain.

Chapter 11

The Roundup

A FEW DAYS LATER, I WATCHED AS A HELICOPTER ROSE above the distant desert ridges. Like a dragonfly defending its territory, it dipped low and hovered, then darted left and right. I saw dust rising from what I knew were the hooves of running wild horses. A helicopter roundup had begun. Wild horses, most still grazing on the mountaintop because of the warm weather, were suddenly pushed off the meadows on a run that would end twenty miles farther at the base of the mountain. Roundups fascinate some people; they love to watch the flowing manes and flying legs of wild horses. I don't see it that way. I see it as robbing wild horses of what they value most, family and freedom.

Dozens of watchers assembled on a ridge top about a quarter of a mile away from the corrals, hidden behind brown cloth called jute. "Get down, get behind the jute," a Bureau of Land

A long run over rocky trails is hard on the
muscles and feet of any foal, even one who
is three and a half months old like Little

Cloud was.

Management (BLM) employee warned as wild horses neared the wings of a trap. Wide at its mouth, the trap's wings gradually narrow until the opening is scarcely wider than the gate of the capture corral.

As the helicopter flew low on the heels of terrified horses, a Judas horse was released to lead the social animals the final hundred yards or so into the corral. Of Biblical origin, the name Judas horse is apt, for this horse unknowingly betrays his species. Trusting the Judas, who has been taught to head for the corrals, the wild horses unwittingly follow—not to freedom but to captivity. It is a clever, insidious technique that works nearly every time.

As the bands streamed in one after another, I saw the Judas horse streak by Cloud's mother, the palomino, who was leading Diamond and the rest of her band. Instead of following the Judas horse, the mare veered away as if to say, *I've been here before and I know this is a trap*. She ran up a sandy hill with her band close behind. Before she could crest the hill, the helicopter pilot instantly spun, tipping the cockpit nose down until the chopper was vertical to the ground. It was a brilliant maneuver. He headed the palomino off, driving her and the band back toward the corrals where they were jammed into a dusty enclosure with twenty other horses.

Little Cloud and Shaman's entire family were driven into a corral with several other bands. I watched the pale colt as he leaned his head next to his mother's. His eyes were half closed; he was tired. When his mother walked to the other side of the corral, however, he followed her with difficulty. When she stopped, he stopped and lifted one back foot in the air, then the other. "Foot sore," I whispered, hoping that was all that was wrong. A long run over rocky trails is hard on the muscles and feet of any foal, even one who is three and a half months old like Little Cloud was. Many, including Flint, were much younger.

 *I watched them race through the trap wings and into the corral with Flint following far behind.*

As the days passed and most of the mountaintop bands had been captured, I wondered if Cloud and his family might escape the roundup. The helicopter pilot told me he had brought Cloud's band partway down Tillet Ridge three times. But when he flew off to bring others along with them, the band had vanished into the dense forest, only to appear back up on the mountaintop. I knew he was determined to bring in the band because Cloud's new mare and both new yearlings were targeted for sale.

The next day, the pilot was successful. I watched Cloud running toward the trap. Later I learned that on the pilot's fourth try, when he focused on Cloud's band alone for the entire long run down to the corrals, he was successful. I watched them race through the trap wings and into the corral with Flint following far behind. The band was divided—Cloud's new mare and the two yearling fillies were taken from him—over Cloud's loud objections. Again and again he whinnied and the females answered back. A whinny is a location call so horses separated from their family can reunite. No matter how much they whinnied, this family would never be together again.

 *Cloud's stunning black father, Raven, was released less one mare who was kept for sale.*

 Chapter 12

Flint's Battle

LATER IN THE DAY, THE PUBLIC WAS ALLOWED TO VIEW the horses so I visited the pens. As I stared in at Cloud and his family, now reduced by half, I was shocked at what I saw. Cloud, the yearling, and Sitka walked to the other end of their corral, leaving Flint standing alongside the wooden fence. The colt turned and looked at them. Then he struggled to take a step. Unlike Little Cloud who was slow, Flint fought just to move his legs. He was stiff and sore on all four feet. He hobbled to Cloud and his mother and sister. It hurt to watch him try to walk. At only two months of age his tender bones and feet simply couldn't hold up to two days of up and down travel plus one long gallop down a rocky trail. In all, he had run thirty miles, perhaps far more, but the idea of being left behind would not have occurred to him. The little *grulla* refused to give up, despite the terrible toll the journey had exacted.

 101

Flint was stiff and sore on all
four feet. He hobbled to Cloud
and his mother and sister.

Within a few days, all the horses who were not going to be auctioned off were released in their family groups. Most bands had experienced losses, a yearling male or female here and there or even an adult mare. Almost every bachelor captured was retained for sale.

Of the dozens of roundups held around the West each year, only the Arrowhead roundup humanely keeps family bands together while in captivity—and upon release—to preserve the integrity of the family unit. Elsewhere, females and males are separated on capture. Old band stallions, some who have spent a lifetime creating a family unit, are released, not with their mares but with other stallions. These old males might never be able to reclaim their family or form a new one.

Cloud's younger brother Red Raven was set free with his mare, Blue Sioux, and their sandy roan foal. Blue Sioux's yearling male, the son of Plenty Coups, was kept for sale. Red Raven stuck protectively close to his mare as they ran by me and my camera, hidden behind a jute curtain. Cloud's stunning black father, Raven, was released less one mare who was kept for sale. Little Cloud, his soreness much improved, was given his freedom with his mother, Shaman, Cedar, and the dun mare. The dun mare's two-year-old daughter was kept for sale. I watched as Little Cloud and the band disappeared into the desert. Through my binoculars, I strained to follow the last puffs of dust raised by their flying hooves. "Going home," I whispered in relief. They were the lucky ones. Cloud's band remained confined—locked in a wooden corral.

It had been weeks since their capture and Flint was still stiff, hardly able to walk. This was not just foot soreness, but something far more serious. Portable X-ray equipment was brought in and fortunately revealed the colt had no broken bones. That was good news. Vets worked on him daily, struggling with him to soak his back left foot. It was believed he had a bad abscess. Epsom salts might draw

Flint was still stiff, hardly able to walk. This was not just foot soreness, but something far more serious.

the infection out to drain, relieving the tremendous pressure. If he didn't improve, humane euthanasia would be considered.

Rather than have him killed, I offered to give him a home in Colorado on my ranch. He might always be crippled, but he could live with Trace and my two Spanish mustangs. The BLM agreed that if he could not improve enough to be released with his family but was fit enough to be assured some quality of life, they would let me take him. Otherwise, he would be put down. *Oh, Flint*, I choked as I walked far enough away from the corrals so no one could see me. I stood alone on a hill. The thought of Flint losing his life was too much for me to bear. *Not lively, fun-loving Flint*. I burst into tears.

A few days later the auction took place. Cloud paced nervously as the public address system blared. Forty-six horses were sold and hauled away, leaving Cloud and his family completely alone in the huge complex of corrals. Flint was still stiff but seemed to be putting a bit more weight on the foot. Was it just my imagination? "No," the local vet, Lyle Bischoff, told me. "He is better." With the help of the soakings, the infection had worked its way to the surface, burst from a hole just above the hoof, and drained from the sole of his hoof as well. Lyle told me Flint had a good chance to recover.

 *Cloud and his little family were free.*

Chapter 13

Freedom

THREE DAYS LATER ON A WARM, CLEAR MORNING, Cloud raced around the big corral. Isolated from his family, he frantically whinnied for them. He had already lost his new mare and two yearling fillies. Now he must have felt he was losing the rest. *Patience, boy,* I silently spoke. *It's going to be all right.*

BLM wild horse manager, Linda Coates-Markle, struggled to restrain a lively Flint, pinning him against the corner of an adjacent corral. I could hear her murmuring, "It's OK, baby. We don't mind the spunkiness at all." Justin Rodgers, a seasonal BLM employee, held Flint's leg up while Lyle finished wrapping the hoof in gauze and what seemed like miles of tape. "How long do you figure this will last?" I asked, referring to the heavily bandaged hoof. "Just a day or two at best," Lyle answered. "You can let his foot down now, Justin," he instructed, and then Linda let the colt go.

Flint stood in the corner of the corral and whinnied. Cloud immediately answered.

Within a half hour the family was reunited and the corral gates swung open. Cloud and his little family were free—steady Sitka trotted out with Flint, who was gamely trying to cling to her side. Cloud and the yearling filly bolted, bucking and running like kids on the last day of school. Then, inexplicably, Cloud stopped. He turned toward his former prison. Head held high, he suddenly pivoted and galloped toward his family, giving one huge defiant kick in the direction of the corrals. No other horse so clearly expressed his attitude about confinement and his exuberance at being set free.

As Cloud's family passed my hiding place behind the jute curtain, I could tell that Flint was doing his very best to keep up with his mother, and that every step caused him pain. Once they had passed, I ran to the top of a sandy hill and watched the four grow smaller and smaller in the vastness of the red hills. Sitka was in the lead, followed by her daughter. Some distance back was Flint then Cloud. The lame colt hobbled up the trail with Cloud following close behind, as if giving encouragement.

The trail to the top of the mountain is nearly twenty miles long, through the red desert, up Sykes Ridge, through the dense forest, and onto the meadows. *Could Flint make it?* I wondered.

Head held high, Cloud suddenly pivoted and galloped toward his family, giving one huge defiant kick in the direction of the corrals.

I saw Shaman and his
family with Little Cloud.
The pale colt seemed fine.

The next day, I drove up Sykes Ridge looking for Cloud and his band. *Such big country and such big empty landscapes*, I mused. I didn't see a single horse on Sykes, which wasn't surprising. I didn't know of any water down there. Near the top of the mountain in an open forest of limber pines, I saw bands of horses, including Cloud's palomino mother and her band. They grazed near little patches of snow remaining from the storm a month before. Grass in and around the edges of the snow was moist, and the palomino pushed her nose into the shallow drift and clipped off some grass with her front teeth.

Clark's nutcrackers in the trees above were collecting pine nuts to cache, calling as they flew from tree to tree. In the distance, I saw Shaman and his family with Little Cloud. They were climbing down a rocky trail into the teacup bowl. The pale colt seemed fine. In a side meadow near the spot where Konik had died, I found Red Raven, Blue Sioux, and the sandy-colored filly. The mare and stallion were grooming each other. Some stallions and mares have an obvious attachment and this was certainly the case with Red Raven and Blue Sioux.

In the open meadows near Penn's Cabin I spotted Cloud, Sitka, and her daughter. At first I didn't see Flint. As I got closer, however, I noticed him lying in the golden grass at Cloud's feet. *He's made it!* I silently cheered. Less than a hundred yards away was a juvenile coyote hunting grasshoppers, leaping into the air as if pouncing on a speedy mouse rather than an insect. As I got to within a hundred yards of Cloud, the coyote looked up at me but continued to hunt, moving ever closer to Cloud. Flint looked over at the coyote, struggled to his feet, and stood under Cloud's head holding his left foot in the air. Neither Cloud nor the coyote seemed to pay any attention to each other or to me. By then, I was only a few hundred feet away. *Naïve little coyote*, I thought. People with

At first I didn't see Flint. As I got closer, however, I noticed him lying in the golden grass at Cloud's feet.

guns travel to the Arrowheads, where it is open season on coyotes 365 days a year. To survive, coyotes must quickly develop a healthy fear of humans.

Flint looked over to his mother, who was perhaps forty feet away. He started toward her, walking haltingly and limping badly. Sitka was sunbathing in the dry grass, but when Flint pawed her back, she got up immediately and let him nurse. Cloud walked toward the little coyote and I thought he might run him off. But the stallion stopped, smelled a stud pile, and started to graze. Apparently he considered the coyote harmless to Flint. I was certain that Cloud and Sitka regarded other predators as lethal. They needed to be particularly vigilant, for Flint could not outrun a mountain lion—not now, perhaps not ever.

 *Fields of brown grass were dotted with snow drifts and the horses favored the sunny, sheltered slopes.*

 Chapter 14

Life and Death

By EARLY NOVEMBER, SNOW BLANKETED THE mountain then mostly melted in a late version of Indian summer. The sun was warm but the wind was a biting reminder that winter could reclaim the mountaintop any day now. Fields of brown grass were dotted with snow drifts and the horses favored the sunny, sheltered slopes.

At the very top of Sykes Ridge, I saw Cloud's little filly with King. Queen was nowhere to be seen. As I walked closer, I was saddened by the horrible condition of the foal. On legs no bigger around than walking sticks, she followed the old stallion. Her fuzzy brown foal coat was dropping out in patches, revealing a stunted body of skin and bones beneath. Yet even near-starvation could not kill the light inside her, and I marveled at her ferocious will to live. I turned away with tears in my eyes and began to search for her

 *Queen had likely slipped on the snow-covered rocks above and fallen to her death.*

mother. The mare was nowhere around so I widened my search.

Behind Penn's Cabin, a sharp vertical drop-off of a hundred feet or more ends in a narrow, tree-lined valley. As I walked the windy rim, I spotted a gray shape at the base of the cliffs and carefully crawled down the slick rocks. The shape I had seen was the body of Queen lying on her side. A bit of blood was dried in her nostrils. The mare had likely slipped on the snow-covered rocks above and fallen to her death. "I'm sorry girl," I whispered as I lightly stroked her gray ear. Her struggle was over. I only wished I could say the same for her little filly.

After hiking out of the valley, I pulled out my cell phone and called the BLM to tell them what had happened and to plead for an emergency adoption for the foal. My request was denied. I did not disagree with the policy of letting nature take its course, but it was just too difficult to ignore her suffering. I never saw Cloud's filly again.

The next day I hiked across the meadows to a high point, where twisted limber pines cling to a rocky cliff. I could see a bit of muddy water in the snow-fed water hole. Beyond it on open slopes I spotted horses, including two white ones, some distance apart. I knew it was Little Cloud with Shaman, and Cloud with his family. I studied Cloud's group, but scattered trees blocked my view. I did not see Flint. He could be there I told myself, unwilling to accept any more tragedy. He could be hidden behind a little tree. I began the daunting hike across the deep ravine.

Shaman's band was closer and I could quickly assess Little Cloud—he was beautiful in his fluffy, nearly white coat. He looked so like his father; strange that there were such stark differences in their personalities. Little Cloud was such a serious, quiet colt.

Standing near the top of the hill, Cloud intently watched bachelor stallions on the opposite hillside. That's when I spotted

Flint standing just behind Sitka. As he walked forward, I saw he was not only quite alive, but he was barely limping! What a tough colt. He, too, displayed a wonderful thick winter coat that exaggerated his refined little head. He walked confidently over to a sandy roan foal just his size. This was strange. She looked like Red Raven's foal. She *was* Red Raven's foal. Blue Sioux was just a few yards away. Both were clearly in Cloud's band. What a surprise! Red Raven, Blue Sioux, and the filly had been one of the closest families on the mountain.

Cloud stepped forward and pounded a hoof, tossing his head in annoyance. Below him, standing in a little gully filled with snow was Red Raven. He stood motionless, watching Cloud. When Cloud took a few steps forward, Red Raven turned and joined the small herd of bachelors on the opposite slope. Blue Sioux watched her roan stallion attentively. Flint sidled up to the sandy roan filly and tried to rub his head on her side in a playful way. The filly walked immediately away and stood next to her mother. This would prove difficult for Cloud. The pair did not want to be a part of Cloud's family.

I felt sad for Red Raven. Whether there was any sibling rivalry at play here, I couldn't say. He and Cloud certainly knew each other as brothers. They grew up together under the tutelage of Raven; the black stallion's blood flows through both their veins. As Red Raven began play-fighting with a bachelor Cloud moved into

 *Shaman's band was closer and I could quickly assess Little Cloud—he was beautiful in his fluffy, nearly white coat.*

As Red Raven began play-fighting with a bachelor Cloud moved into action, snaking his expanded family far down the valley, away from Red Raven.

action, snaking his expanded family far down the valley, away from Red Raven. I left the mountain a few days later. A million thoughts and emotions rattled around in my head in sync with my teeth-jarring ride down the bumpy road.

Later, when snows forced the horses to abandon the mountaintop, I lost track of Cloud.

 *In February, I tried another strategy. Maybe*
Cloud and his band weren't on Sykes Ridge.
Maybe I could find them in the red desert.

 Chapter 15

The Red Desert

MONTHS PASSED WITHOUT A SIGHTING OF CLOUD on Sykes Ridge. By January, little snow had fallen, but it was enough to block Sykes Ridge Road in the dark, narrow passageways through Cougar Canyon. I hiked in the places I'd seen him the year before near the mouth of the canyon but saw no horses. I drove up on Tillet Ridge and with my spotting scope I combed the ridges of distant Sykes. I was focusing on what looked like a *grulla* and a dun when a white colt trotted through the frame and disappeared into a thick cover of Douglas firs. "Little Cloud," I said out loud. The white colt was unmistakable. *What a lucky sighting,* I thought. Only two seconds later and I wouldn't have seen any of them.

Hours passed and my eyes were giving out. I saw more horses but not the white stallion I was looking for. Cloud remained elusive. He was nearly impossible to find in winter.

Trace and I followed the horse trail into the gradually widening canyon.

In February, I tried another strategy. Maybe Cloud and the band weren't on Sykes Ridge. Maybe I could find them in the red desert and figured it was worth a try. So Trace and I traveled from Colorado and together began the search for Cloud. Just as water holes are the best places to look for horses in summer, springs in the desert are good places to look in winter.

The most isolated yet centrally located of three springs in the Arrowheads is Cottonwood, aptly named for the grove surrounding it. The spring is just a trickle that drips from the side of a wash. The steady rivulet fills a shallow pool only a few inches deep and a dozen feet across. The spring is a modest but reliable source of water. Around the spring, imprinted in the mud and sand, were the cloven hooves of mule deer and the distinctive tracks of a cottontail hopping to and from the water and the cover of brush.

Big and small horse tracks lined the muddy bank and led into a canyon. Trace and I followed the horse trail into the gradually widening canyon. Flash floods had taken out parts of the sand banks. Limbs and stumps, deposited when the torrent subsided, were tangled into piles on shrubby sand bars. It was quiet, save for the sound of Trace's footfalls on the sandy trail. We were following a kind of salmon-colored horse highway. Tracks crisscrossed each other, going in both directions. We rounded a sharp curve where canyon walls gave way to wide sage-covered slopes. Trace stopped and raised his neck straight up in the air. It was his giraffe pose, and I knew what it meant. Something was out there.

I looked where he looked and saw a herd of mule deer a hundred yards away. They were moving slowly away but keeping us in their sights. *It pays to be wary*, I thought. Mountain lions prowl the desert and an inattentive deer could easily become lunch. I believe the cats follow the seasonal mule deer migration, moving up the mountain in summer and down in winter.

Farther into the canyon, red rock walls loomed above Trace and me on both sides. *Great place for an ambush*, I thought, glancing up at the cliffs and rocks above. The trail veered to the right, then uphill. Fresh tracks led up a steep grade onto a gravelly dry flat. We took the cutoff and topped the grade. That's where we saw Cloud staring at us. My hunch had paid off. I wondered how long he had been standing up there watching. He returned to his family as Trace and I approached from several hundred yards. I stopped and waved as I always did. *Here I am. It's just me. Nothing to fear.* Still, the band moved away slowly, so Trace and I stayed put. I didn't want Cloud to feel we were pressuring him.

Wait a minute, something wasn't right! I suddenly noticed Sitka was missing. Flint was there, his older sister, and Blue Sioux and her daughter, whom I had begun calling Sand. They all looked fine. But where was Sitka? We followed the band as they meandered toward the big red buttes. They stopped in a sandy wash and foraged. All the time, I kept a sharp lookout for Sitka and anything unusual—flocks of ravens or magpies, or the pungent smell of decaying flesh. Every once in a while I felt like I was getting a whiff of something foul, but it could very well have been my imagination.

As I continued to search, I spotted a big band of horses. Trace stood perfectly still while I pulled out my binoculars and glassed. It was the biggest band to live in this part of the red desert year round. The group's stallion was Starbuck, a beautiful dun with a star. Sitka was definitely not among Starbuck's group. And scanning the entire area, I didn't see any other horses.

I rode to within a hundred yards of Cloud, dismounted, and sat on a rock. Trace draped his head over my shoulder, and I rubbed his face. Together we watched. I was trying to detect any sign of nervousness or anxiety from the band. They acted fine, at least as fine as they could down here where they had to dig for

I suddenly noticed Sitka was missing.

Cloud grabbed little tufts of sparse yellow grass, clipping it off at the ground with his front teeth.

roots and scrounge on weeds. Flint was munching on a big tumble-weed; it seemed more like something to do than something to eat. *Where is your mother, boy?* I silently asked.

Cloud grabbed little tufts of sparse yellow grass, clipping it off at the ground with his front teeth. *Why did you bring them here, Cloud?* He snaked Blue Sioux closer to Flint, Sand, and the yearling. *Ah, maybe I do know why you're down here.* My mind continued to ramble. *You took Blue Sioux to the one place where Red Raven might not find you, huh?* I thought this was a distinct possibility. *But did you lose Sitka in the process?*

The next day I rode Trace in a wide swath around Cloud and the band. I looked for other horse bands, scanned the flats for irregular shapes, checked gullies, and looked under small trees for a body I hoped I wouldn't find. Then it began to snow, then blow; looking for horses became impossible. I was fairly certain of only one thing—if Sitka were dead, there would be no Cloud colt this year.

Over the next few days, whenever Cloud spotted Red Raven he would rush out and spar with him, but ever so briefly.

Chapter 16

The Survivor

IN EARLY MAY, I RETURNED TO THE ARROWHEADS. FIRST
I stopped and searched for horses in the red desert, thinking Cloud
might still be down there. Starbuck and his band were out on a gravelly flat, not far from where I had spotted them several months
before. I scanned the group carefully looking for Sitka, but she
wasn't there. I feared the mare was dead but hoped she had been
stolen by another stallion and I might still find her alive and well. I
watched the flats for a little while longer, tracking any movement.
Cloud could be here, I thought. It's only luck to catch a glimpse of the
very horses you're looking for.

Down in Cougar Canyon there was a bit of snow, but not
enough to stop me. I slipped my Expedition into four-wheel drive,
low gear, and began the climb out of the canyon. I stopped on a high
point where I have often glassed for horses. Startled by the four-

wheeler, a flock of rosy finches chirped brightly as they flew out of the junipers. The winds were still light as they often were in the morning. There was a greater chance the bands would be out on the ridge tops rather than tucked away on the side slopes. As I scanned one fingerlike ridge after another, I spotted a dun horse. Where there was one horse, there might be more. This one could be Shaman or his dun mare.

I saw a few other bands even farther up on Sykes, but they were clearly not Cloud's family. Sometimes I have overlooked a horse standing very close to me in my haste to scan far away. This was the case with the old stallion, King, whom I finally spotted grazing in a gully not fifty yards to my left. He had survived another winter, but I believed that the coming summer could be his last. *What a grand old horse*, I thought. I hoped he would join up with Old Blackie, another former band stallion, so they could hang out together and buoy each other's spirits.

As I climbed one of the final hills before the open Sykes's meadows, I saw something light on the hilltop, stopped the car, and whipped out my binoculars. Often I have tried to turn light rocks or bleached tree trunks into a pale stallion, but today I found the real thing. It was Cloud! He was in plain sight on top of a ridge. Beside him were Flint, Blue Sioux, Sand, and Sitka's daughter. Below them, walking on the side slope was another horse. Peering through my binoculars I got the most wonderful view of a blue roan. *Sitka?!* As

I'm sure I did a double take for in Sitka's flank area, just in front of her back leg, a huge lump protruded.

132

she walked on, the band descended the hill and fell in line behind her. Definitely, it was Sitka. I could hardly believe it and hurried to catch up with them. Cloud's family topped the main ridgeline and crossed into a forest on the edge of the cliff overlooking the Big Horn River.

Grabbing my camera gear, I excitedly started after them. *Sitka is back!* I wanted to yell. I felt like it was my birthday and Christmas all rolled into one. Snow was piled under trees at the edge of the cliff and that was where Sitka had led them. By the time I caught up, she was already taking huge bites of snow that dribbled out of her mouth. *Where have you been, girl?* I silently asked. I wished she could have told me for I had absolutely no clues to help me out.

She had what looked like an old cut on her head. The hair hadn't grown back, but the old wound was just a white line. She had shed out on her head, shoulders, and rump, but not around her middle, which was white and fuzzy. No one else in the band was looking his or her best yet either. Flint's coat was a dry pale brown, but I knew it would eventually be replaced with a handsome *grulla* coat. Even Cloud looked a bit ratty. His coat was nearly shed out, except for a bit of white hair on his rump, and his hipbones stuck out a little. I sat and watched the raggedy ensemble chewing on the snow and making that funny choking sound as melted snow poured out their noses.

Bachelors were playing hundreds of yards off, yet Cloud took out after them—not to play but to run them out of the country.

Cloud may have felt it was only a matter of time before Red Raven would try to win back his family.

Beyond the horses, the blue-green ribbon that was the Bighorn River meandered through the canyon thousands of feet below. A junco sang from the trees just over their heads, and I could hear the distinctive nasal call of a white-breasted nuthatch not too far away. The high three-note mating whistle of a nearby chickadee rose and fell and was answered by a prospective mate. It was starting to sound like spring.

I looked back at Cloud's family just as Sitka turned her right side toward me. I'm sure I did a double take for in her flank area, just in front of her back leg, a huge lump protruded. As I stared at the lump, it appeared to move. *Could it be a foal moving?* I wondered. *Maybe this was the colt's head?* Although foals change position a few weeks before birth, this just didn't look right to me at all. The mare acted as though she felt fine, but her condition was a troubling turn of events, and one I would fret about for months to come.

Later in the day, the band wandered back onto the open ridges as Cloud continually snaked them together. When he saw a black band stallion a quarter of a mile away, he shook his head in agitation and then galloped out to confront him. Both stallions screamed and reared, pawing the air in a serious-looking duel. *What's the big deal?* I wondered silently. Cloud raced back to the band and snaked them farther away. Bachelors were playing hundreds of yards off, yet Cloud took out after them—not to play but to run them out of the country. Again, he rushed back to the band and this time he snaked them the other way! This seemingly erratic behavior went on for days before I discovered why Cloud was so agitated.

The band had moved out onto the crest of a ridge, and Cloud stared downhill into a ravine. I went to see if I could tell what he was looking at. Red Raven was walking below. He stopped and looked up at Cloud. No wonder Cloud was anxious. His little brother had not stopped pining for his family. Cloud may have felt it was only a matter of time until Red Raven would try to win them back. That unnerved him. The roan didn't make a move toward Blue Sioux and Sand. Rather, he drifted toward Big Coulee and dropped out of sight.

Over the next few days, whenever Cloud spotted Red Raven he would rush out and spar with him, but ever so briefly. The roan would trot off with the bachelors, unable or unwilling to do battle with his older brother.

What had transformed Little Cloud? He was

so much bolder than I had ever seen him.

Chapter 17

Becoming Bolder

As I watched Cloud's drama unfolding, I kept track of Shaman's band as well. The two families were often close enough for me to watch at the same time. The golden dun stallion shone like a bright copper penny on the crests of the ridges. Shaman had shed out and looked sleek and fit, as did the others in his band. They had wintered well, better than Cloud's band had in the desert. Little Cloud had grown taller, but like most of the yearlings and foals he still sported a fluffy winter coat. Youngsters are generally slower to shed out than their parents. That's nature's way of protecting them from spring weather that can turn cold and damp.

I spotted a stallion, mare, and yearling far out on a ridge. Through my binoculars I could identify the red roan stallion known as The Rev, in honor of Lutheran minister Floyd Schwieger. It was Schwieger and other local activists who fought to save the

 *Little Cloud had grown taller, but like most of the yearlings and foals he still sported a fluffy winter coat.*

Arrowhead herd from a government plan to remove the horses forty years ago. Without the minister and other supporters such as Hope Ryden, a TV correspondent with ABC News, the wild horses of the Arrowheads would most likely be a fading memory.

I observed The Rev, his lone mare, and their yearling son as they moved closer to Shaman's family. I named The Rev's black yearling PK, for Preacher's Kid. When Little Cloud saw PK, he trotted over to him, grabbed him by the back of the neck, and began shaking. The black colt retaliated and dove for Little Cloud's legs. The white colt swiveled, landing a firm kick to PK's side. Then the two started racing in circles, suddenly slid to a stop, reared up, and bit at each other. They took a short break then started the whole biting, rearing, and running game all over again.

Over the course of nearly a week, I watched Little Cloud in amazement as he pranced around with his tail in the air and his head held high. On several occasions he would march right over to Cloud's band and try to engage Flint in play. Flint would turn his butt to Little Cloud, kick him in the chest, then walk away. How the tables had turned. As a colt, Flint could hardly stand still and Little Cloud had been the sickly and lackluster one. I was certain that Flint's injury had made him more cautious. In time, I hoped, Flint will regain his strength and spirit. Unexplained was the sudden change in Little Cloud. Along with the deep blue alpine forget-me-knots on the dry hilltops, the colt, too, had blossomed.

Little Cloud sauntered back to his mother like a cocky teenager. Yet when he returned to her, he began to nurse like a foal. Little Cloud would be a year old in less than two months and was only a few inches shorter than his mother. Nevertheless, she allowed him to suckle. Her receptiveness was a sign she would not foal this year. Otherwise, she would have weaned her big baby months ago.

Over the course of nearly a week, I watched Little Cloud in amazement as he pranced around with his tail in the air and his head held high.

Late one afternoon, PK and Little Cloud were back at play, racing across the rim of a hill with the shadow of Tillet Ridge as background. The setting sun shone through their flying manes and tails, and dust rose under their dancing hooves. *What had transformed Little Cloud?* He was so much bolder than I had ever seen him. I had never really been satisfied with the name Little Cloud—the dashing colt deserved better. *What would be a good name for you?* I pondered. All of a sudden it seemed obvious. He had become so bold that he named himself. *Bolder!* And that is what I have called him ever since.

 *Out in the open meadow, Red Raven was*

standing behind Blue Sioux.

Chapter 18

Red Raven's
Revenge

A LARGE HERD OF BIGHORN SHEEP RAMS WERE roaming the lower slopes of Sykes Ridge in early June when I returned. Some were young males with horns barely making a curl while others were older, their magnificent horns wrapping in an arc around their faces. I've often spotted bighorn sheep on Sykes during late spring, but I have never found wild horse bands here in June.

Cloud's, Shaman's, and The Rev's bands were grazing on Sykes, not two hundred yards from the rams. Typically the horses migrate to the top of the mountain in spring where there is good grazing and water. There are no water holes here and with the snowbanks melted, I wondered how the horses could survive. All seemed well enough except Sitka, whose abdominal lump was protruding even more. Flint, Bolder, and PK had half shed their winter coats and were looking really ratty, while the mares and stallions

147

appeared shiny and sleek in their short summer coats. But why weren't they in the high meadows with green grass and plenty of water?

Each day I drove down from Penn's Cabin and each day the three bands were still grazing on Sykes. I couldn't figure it out. I studied Bolder as he flaunted his newfound personality. He was growing stronger and had eclipsed PK and Flint in size. These three were some of the only male yearlings to survive a foal season in which nearly a third were killed by mountain lions or had otherwise died.

Shaman's dun mare had given birth to a lovely sorrel filly I named Splash for her star and dribble of white below it. The foal loved to dash through the sage, dodging, jumping, and bucking. She took a particular liking to Bolder and was fond of following him around. He would lay his ears back and bump against her playfully. She seemed to love it and danced around the big yearling.

Cloud had gained weight and was looking quite handsome in his off-white, unscarred coat. His band seemed content to nibble at the little bit of grass left on Sykes. Blue Sioux looked far along in her pregnancy—her sides bulged out so far that I imagined her accidentally getting wedged between two trees. She foaled about this same time last year, so she was due any day. *How strange to see them here. Where were they finding water?* I wondered.

Bolder would lay his ears back and bump against Splash playfully.

Every evening I drove up onto the mountain where all the other horses were enjoying the tender new shoots of grass. Diamond had two new foals in his band. The palomino had a filly over a month old by the looks of her, and the dun mare had a pale dun colt only a week or so old. The two foals seemed to count the seconds to sunset, when they would begin to rip around the meadows, bucking and racing. First the filly would start, then the little colt would follow, kicking as he ran.

The next morning I looked around up top and spotted The Rev, his mare, and PK near the snow-fed water hole. They had finally come. Maybe this would be the day Cloud and Shaman brought their families to the high meadows, too. As I headed back down the mountain, I noticed Red Raven just west of Penn's Cabin—all alone. I felt sorry for the young stallion and wondered if Cloud was hiding out on Sykes just to avoid his younger brother.

Miles down on Sykes Ridge, Cloud was easy to find, grazing with the band on an open hilltop. I immediately noticed that Blue Sioux was missing. *She must have gone off to foal*, I thought. *How exciting!* Red Raven's yearling filly, Sand, looked for her mother every so often and whinnied. "She'll be back soon, girl," I whispered. Cloud walked off from the band and stood staring out at wooded hillsides. It was mid-morning and I believed the mare would be back any minute.

 *It was nearly dark by the time I abandoned my vigil and drove back up to Penn's Cabin.*

By noon I decided I couldn't sit still any longer and began to hike around the band, searching for, and expecting to see, a new baby. I found deer on the forested side slopes and could hear a woodpecker pounding on a dead tree in the groves. I checked on Cloud often to see if the mare had returned. The afternoon slipped away with Cloud's band staying in one small area the entire time.

It was nearly dark by the time I abandoned my vigil and drove back up to Penn's Cabin. In the dying light I saw that King had joined up with Old Blackie. *Wonderful*, I thought. The two old stallions would keep each other company. *Goodnight, old fellows.*

The next morning at about 6:30, golden light flooded the high green meadows. I brushed my teeth outside the cabin as I always did. Half a dozen chipmunks kept me company, sitting on a woodpile a few feet away. I walked out on the hilltop in front of Penn's Cabin. Diamond's band was below me, side-lit in the early morning light. Cloud's palomino mother was nursing her foal while she groomed with her yearling filly. If there was a better mother among the fifty or so mares on the Arrowheads, I don't know who she was. The palomino was affectionate and attentive, and she produced an abundance of milk.

I walked across the crest of the hill, moving toward the snow-fed water hole. I was astonished by what I discovered. Out in the open meadow, Red Raven was standing behind Blue Sioux. Lying at their feet was a newborn foal. *How did this happen?* The question repeated itself over and over in my brain. Cloud had never fought Red Raven. How could he? Red Raven had never left the mountaintop. Before I drove down the mountain to find Cloud, I had seen Red Raven on top—alone.

Blue Sioux's tail was still wet from giving birth no more than an hour or two ago, I guessed. It took me a few minutes to connect the dots in this amazing drama. The closeness of the stal-

The foal nuzzled his mother's side, trying to find warm milk. Within a few seconds he was suckling.

lion and mare was evident. All along Cloud had appeared paranoid about losing her—and Red Raven had not given up on getting her back. Blue Sioux never bonded with Cloud and wanted to leave. That part I had figured out. The rest was completely unpredictable.

I have concluded that the mare left Cloud at the only time he would let her go. He must have believed she was going off to foal and, indeed, she had. *What a clever mare!* I reasoned. I visualized her walking confidently away from the band. Then she just kept going. She walked miles up the mountain. This would not have been without danger. She ran the risk of a band stallion chasing her, trying to add her to his band. Even worse, bachelors might have fought over her. In either case, she could have been injured. Regardless, she risked everything to come back to Red Raven.

Their foal must have been born in the predawn hours when the sky was a dull gray. I'm sure Red Raven was standing guard. It is commonly believed that mares go off alone to foal and that is probably true in the majority of cases. But I have seen a number of instances in which the mare stayed within a few yards of her family to give birth.

The foal began to wake up. He pushed himself up on sturdy but wobbly knees. Then he paused and nearly tipped over before hoisting himself upright. The foal was a male and very light eyed. He took a few stiff, uncertain steps forward as his father pulled his lips away from his teeth and inhaled Blue Sioux's scent. Then the mare and stallion did something that may not have been seen or filmed before in the wild. Red Raven moved confidently up behind his mare. She kicked at him with one leg then backed into him, and they bred.

It took me a while to process these unbelievable events. The mare was not in heat. On the contrary, she would not be in estrous for another week or more. And it's believed that horses don't breed outside a heat cycle. Well, these two were living proof that horses do copulate for reasons other than reproduction.

The foal tottered to his mother. She reached down and gently touched his head. Red Raven stood just a few feet away. The foal nuzzled his mother's side, trying to find warm milk. Within a few seconds he was suckling.

I felt pulled in two directions. I was sorry for Cloud and for Sand, now without her mother. But I was happy for Blue Sioux and Red Raven. I left them alone and returned to Penn's where I packed the car to drive down onto Sykes Ridge. I still had a mystery to unravel and I was determined to solve it.

 *Bolder's mother was the first to turn tail and run, followed by her son.*

Chapter 19

The Mystery Trail

FAR DOWN ON SYKES I COULD SEE CLOUD AND HIS BAND
on a ridge near the drop-off into Big Coulee. I wondered if there
might be a trail off the cliffs into the canyon. Could that be where
there was water—perhaps a spring down in the canyon?

I spotted Shaman's band much closer to me, standing still
on the spine of the main ridge. Bolder stayed close to his mother as
the family took a few hesitant steps toward a herd of bighorn rams.
Shaman moved out in front of the mares, cautiously assessing the
twenty male bighorns only fifty yards away. When the rams took a
few steps toward the horses, Shaman let out one of his most explo-
sive snorts. Bolder's mother was the first to turn tail and run, followed by her son. The rest of the band followed at a full gallop. This
sudden retreat surprised me. If the two species pay any attention to
each other at all, it is usually the sheep who move away from the

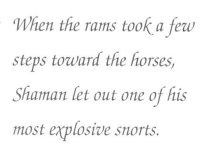 *When the rams took a few steps toward the horses, Shaman let out one of his most explosive snorts.*

horses. I wondered if there was something else bothering them.

When I caught up with them, I sat on the ground watching. They grazed a bit but were uneasy. They stopped and looked at me. *Why are they staring at me?* I waved so they'd know it was me. I'd been sitting there for half an hour. Yet now I'm a threat? Then out of the corner of my eye I saw movement and turned my head slowly. A bear was standing on its hind legs not more than fifty feet away, watching me! Neither of us moved. After a while I tried ever so slowly to lift my still camera off my lap. No luck. I couldn't even begin to get the camera to my eye before the little bear raced off, running on only three legs.

I recognized the crippled bear immediately—the same black bear who three years before had come to eat on the stallion Challenger after he was struck and killed by lightning. Disabled though the little bear was, she had survived. I assumed she was a female, for she was just as small as the last time I had seen her. I figured that the bear had been keeping Shaman's family on edge; the bighorn rams just compounded their unease.

The little bear ran off toward the edge of Bighorn Canyon. I waited a few seconds before giving in to the urge to see where she may have gone and then walked to the rim, where I lost sight of her. I looked over the edge at a two thousand–foot drop-off and the juniper-studded desert below. Unless bears can fly, she didn't step off here. Douglas firs fringed the rim in spots. In fact, there was a dense forest just to my left. Trees grow tall in places where the slopes are not completely vertical. The little bear must have retreated into them.

I walked back and caught a glimpse of Shaman disappearing with his band over a rise and I hustled to catch up. When I saw them next, they were heading toward Bighorn Canyon. The mares were in front, then Bolder and Shaman in the rear. The band was clearly going somewhere, and I had a hunch it was to water. They vanished into trees at the edge of the canyon and I hiked down, confident I would soon find their secret. But they were long gone by the time I got there, with no visible trail in either direction.

I skirted the rim above the canyon, looking down from the cliffs for anything that moved between the trees. I saw something light colored for an instant. It had to be Bolder—or Cloud. I came to a spot where the forest opened up a bit and caught a glimpse of a small patch of white—and the horses approaching it. They stopped and put their heads down. They were eating snow. *Snow?* It seemed impossible, but they were standing at a small mound of snow wedged between trees against the overhanging cliff. Snow here in June during a drought year was unheard of. Still, there it was. As the band munched, I wondered how they had gotten off this cliff and found their way to this hidden patch of snow.

I backtracked and looked for tracks in the direction the horses might have been traveling. I followed a few hoofprints before losing them over solid rock. Then I saw a trail where the cliff dropped into the forest. The trail wound through the trees, ascended, descended, only to ascend and descend again. It passed closer to the cliffs, and then led over a hundred feet away from them. Eventually I spotted Shaman's band moving away. I only got a brief look at Bolder, trotting off down the trail at the end of the

Shaman and his family vanished into trees at the edge of the canyon and I hiked down, confident I would soon find their secret.

single file of horses. From the trail I saw the cliffs, but not a trace of snow. So I backtracked yet again, finding smaller paths off the main trail. One of these small paths led up to the little heap of melting snow. I climbed up and was surprised at just how small the cache of snow was, maybe four by four feet and several feet deep.

Feeling like I had unraveled a mystery, I slumped down and leaned against a tree. How many horses over how many generations (or centuries even) had taught their foals about a secret trail to the last water of spring? The conditions had to be perfect to allow snow to still exist here—very little light, an overhanging ledge, a tree on one side and rocks on two sides. *Nature's refrigerator*, I concluded.

I decided to wait and see if Cloud's family was using this spot, too, and had a lot of time to look around. There were other tracks on the little paths leading to the snow, including what looked like a human's barefoot print. The little bear? It made sense that she came down to escape me and get a little drink at the same time.

A bird, a slender Townsend's solitaire, lit on a low tree limb just at eye level and I could see the soft peach coloration on its gray wings. From some distance away, I could hear the bell-like calls of another and wondered if it was this bird's mate.

Six hours later, long after scattered sunlight had abandoned the little icebox, I heard noises in the forest. *Footfalls?* I stared into the trees for what seemed like a long time. I hoped it was

 *I only got a brief look at Bolder, before he trotted off down the trail at the end of the single file of horses.*

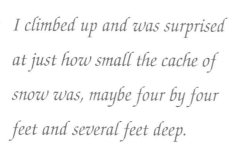 *I climbed up and was surprised*
at just how small the cache of
snow was, maybe four by four
164   *feet and several feet deep.*

horses and not a meat-eating species. Cloud was the first one I saw, smelling leaves and the trail itself as he led the band to snow. He could smell the bear and was cautious. When he saw me he stopped, and I waved. He continued on with Sitka right behind. The two were followed by Sitka's daughter, then Flint, and Sand. All plunged their noses into the snow, grabbing huge bites that dribbled from their mouths. I wondered how long the snow cone stash would last. Sooner, rather than later, they would be forced to join the others atop the mountain.

 *From a distance I could see Cloud's mother*

with Diamond and the band.

Chapter 20

The Secret Garden

Even in the throes of a drought, the high meadows had a brief burst of extravagant color in late June. Green meadows were ablaze with purple lupine, white fuzz-topped bistort, Indian and sulphur paintbrush, and delicate little clumps of buttercups. I found many horse bands in a lovely valley where the snow melts later than it does on the flatter, more exposed meadows. From a distance I could see Cloud's mother with Diamond and the band. Red Raven, his mare, and the foal were not too far from them. A group of bachelors wandered through sage on the far hillside.

As I hiked down, I saw Shaman's band emerge from the forest at a run. *Finally,* I thought, *the snow cone has melted on Sykes.* The whole band was making a dash into the beautiful meadow. Shaman was in the lead, followed by his three mares. Bringing up the rear was Bolder, and then the little sorrel filly, Splash. I was startled at the change in Bolder. In just two weeks he had traded in his fluffy, white winter coat for one of lustrous deep gold. He had become a stunning golden palomino.

Then I saw Cloud and his band running into the valley, too. The pale stallion had put on weight. I knew he was feeling spunky for he pranced, shook his head a bit, and lifted his legs high in the air with every stride. Flint was galloping along behind him. *Was he just a little lame on that back left leg? Maybe a bit*, I thought. What was more noticeable than any limp was his coat, half of which was his light-brown winter coat and the other half his steel-gray summer one. He had yet to completely shed out, which could be a sign of poor health. Still, he looked in good flesh. So did Sand and the two-year-old filly, though they had a remnant of winter hair remaining too.

Sitka trotted along, looking as big as a barn. The mare was extremely far along in her pregnancy. The lump in her flank was huge. How could she possibly have a colt if it was lying sideways? If the lump were the colt's head, could it turn itself around when it came time to be born? This appeared to be a pregnancy gone terribly wrong.

In the distance, a grayish colored coyote loped up a horse trail on the hillside and ambled out of sight. I walked farther into the valley and looked toward the spot where the meadow meets the deep green forests and cliffs of pale yellow limestone. The dark bay band stallion, Mateo, was there with Cloud's sister Electra and her pretty, nearly black filly foal. The filly had what looked like a cascading waterfall mark on her face, so I named her Cascade.

As I walked toward Mateo's band, I saw a new foal lying in a bed of lupine. Even from far away, the foal's *grulla* mother spotted me and took a few anxious steps, her head high in the air and her ears pricked forward to detect the slightest noise. I took a few

I was startled at the change in Bolder. In just two weeks he had traded in his fluffy, white winter coat for one of lustrous deep gold.

more steps, waved, and sat down. In time, she seemed to recognize that I was no threat to the baby.

The foal got up and hobbled to her mother's side to nurse, then plopped down in the flowers and lay flat, basking in the warm sun. The foal was a solid *grulla*, a carbon copy of her mother. After a while, she woke up and struggled to stand again, nursed, then tried to run, hopping over flowers and making a shaky circle around her mother. What a perfect day—warm but not hot, a deep blue sky overhead, and a sea of purple lupine flowers below. I named this secluded spot the Secret Garden. Sheltered from the wind by forested hills and limestone cliffs, it was a grand place to be born.

I watched Mateo rush up the hillside above his family to warn three bachelors to keep their distance. Included in that bachelor band was the son of Cloud's *grulla* mare, Queen. Her two-year-old red dun was a slender colt with a narrow blaze on his face and the elegant lines of a racer. He backed shyly away from Mateo, wanting nothing to do with the stout stallion. I had named the dark bay Mateo, one of the Lakota Sioux words for bear, when he was a young bachelor, hardly older than the red dun. I hoped the young red dun bachelor might one day father foals. In that way the spirit of his parents, King and Queen, might live on for years to come.

Day after day I returned to the Secret Garden to sit with the horses. I followed them when they climbed the steep hillside to go to water. The last evening I was there, I found Cloud above the spring-fed lake playing with half a dozen bachelors. He reared and pawed at them, and they all sprinted then stopped and spun, biting playfully at each other's legs. Even Shaman, who had to be over fifteen now, joined in the jousting match, and Cloud was eager to take him on. Cloud struck out with his front legs in his characteristic one-two punch. Then he spun and kicked out at Shaman's head with his back legs.

The foal was a solid grulla, a carbon copy of
her mother.

By the time I caught up with Cloud, he was
grazing peacefully with Sitka, Flint, Sand,
and the two-year-old filly.

Abruptly, right in the midst of play, Cloud jerked his head up as if he'd forgotten something. He suddenly charged uphill and out of sight. By the time I caught up with him, he was grazing peacefully with Sitka, Flint, Sand, and the two-year-old filly. As the sun dipped behind storm clouds that were building in the west and as faraway bolts of lightning flashed over the distant Beartooth Mountains, I worried about Sitka's condition. But I never dreamed of the danger all of the wild horses would be facing that summer.

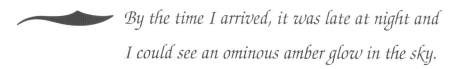 *By the time I arrived, it was late at night and*

I could see an ominous amber glow in the sky.

Chapter 21

The Dragon Awakes

TWO WEEKS LATER, THE PHONE RANG AT 8:00 A.M. My worst nightmare had become reality. A fire had broken out in the Arrowheads. The measured voice on the other end was Trish Kerby, my friend and ally in defending wild horses. "The fire broke out late yesterday afternoon. The cause isn't clear, but it's burning out of control," she continued. I clung to her every word. The horses were in danger.

Within hours I was packed and on the road to Montana. When I arrived, it was late at night and I could see an ominous amber glow in the sky. I turned off the highway and began to wind around on dirt roads. Gravitating like a moth to flame, I was heading toward the source of the fire, Crooked Creek Canyon.

I had driven the difficult winding road alongside Crooked Creek Canyon many times. Although the route to the mountaintop took longer than the road up Tillet Ridge, the spectacular views were worth it. Water erosion and ancient uplifting had crafted the canyon. Its vertical cliffs slice downward to a modest creek, which tumbles five thousand feet from the mountaintop into the desert. The little creek eventually empties into the Bighorn River at the very bottom of the horse range.

A roadblock prevented me from driving to the canyon, so I backtracked to a high point and scrambled up a sandy hilltop. I watched the fire burning dimly only to see it flare up as one tree after another ignited. Sparks shot up into the starry night sky. It was midnight but still hot and there was a breeze, not a good combination to contain a wildfire.

When I left the Arrowheads in late June, the subalpine meadows were so green I had convinced myself that the horse range would avoid fire, even though the west was suffering from another horrible fire season. In the two weeks since I'd left, temperatures had risen into the one hundred degree range. Strong, dry winds sucked every bit of moisture from the air. Lightning had been observed, but not during the five days before the blaze. I speculated that lightning might have struck some time ago, initially igniting only a tiny undetectable fire that smoldered benignly for days. Like a sleeping dragon, it lay dormant until intense heat and high winds breathed life into it. Then it exploded into a four

Then it exploded into a four thousand–acre blaze within a few short hours. The dragon had awakened.

thousand–acre blaze within a few short hours. The dragon had awakened.

The next morning I drove out to the BLM and U.S. Forest Service command center in the desert. An elite Forest Service team had been called in from Idaho. A team spokesman explained that the blaze was simply too hot to safely put firefighters into the canyon; they might never get out. So the fire must be fought on the perimeter and from the air.

Forest Service and BLM fire bosses had flown aerial reconnaissance and knew there were horses nearby. What they didn't know was precisely where the wild horses might go if the fire climbed out of the canyon and into the forests of Tillet then Sykes. I looked at their maps and explained that the horses migrate vertically up and down the mountain, using familiar trails on the two ridges. To get from the top to the bottom, they pass through dense forest littered with enormous amounts of deadfall. If these forests caught fire, the horses could be trapped on top. "But you'll get this thing stopped before then, right?" I smiled anxiously at the official. "That's the plan," he laughed nervously, then added softly, "We're sure going to try."

A helicopter flew over just behind us, water spraying out of the red bucket dangling underneath. Choppers were dipping water from a nearby pond, filling red buckets with hundreds of

I squinted up at Sykes Ridge, but I couldn't see the top. It was engulfed in smoke.

gallons of water at a time. Then they flew into the canyon, looking like small toys suspended against a backdrop of a smoke-choked sky. The five hundred gallons of water dropped into the canyon looked no more effective than a squirt gun against a roaring inferno. Slurry bomber pilots flew half a dozen flights a day over the canyons, expelling magenta clouds of fire retardant from their converted WWII planes.

Despite their efforts, the fire slowly spread. The BLM barricaded the roads into the horse range. The fire was too unpredictable, they concluded, and people could be trapped with no way to escape. Easterly winds combined with low humidity and hot temperatures could send the blaze roaring out of the canyon and onto Tillet Ridge in less than an hour. This worst-case scenario began to unfold. The wind shifted to the east, blowing smoke directly toward the horse range.

I drove over into the Bighorn Canyon on the only open road. From the paved highway I spotted a group of bighorn sheep ewes. Above the ewes on a gravelly slope were four lambs, no bigger than fox terriers. The babies dashed playfully down the rocky hillside. I thought about the bighorn sheep living in Crooked Creek Canyon and hoped they had time to make their way safely out.

I stepped out of the car at the canyon overlook. The wind nearly lifted me off my feet and I grabbed onto the car door. I squinted up at Sykes Ridge, but I couldn't see the top. It was engulfed in smoke. I wondered how the horses could breathe. Was Sitka all right? Had she foaled? I felt so helpless. "Are you all right Cloud?" I whispered. If any horse knew this wilderness and how to avoid disaster, it was Cloud. He grew up on Tillet, he was a bachelor on Sykes, and he wintered in a breathtaking area called Lost Water Canyon. Beautiful Lost Water was burning right now. *Go away wind*, I silently screamed. *At least blow the other way*.

Fearing the fire would reach the horse range, firefighters cut down many of the trees along Tillet Ridge Road to make a fire-break. Even a few feet can make a difference in stopping a wildfire. I guessed that Tillet was the line drawn in the sand, the line on which the firefighters would make their stand. If the blaze breached the road, the horse range could be lost.

The fire continued to grow but at a much slower rate. It had charred seven thousand acres when Mother Nature stepped in. It rained. Not a lot, but it rained that night. The wind died down and the temperature dropped. Now the fire that threatened to climb the canyon walls seemed unable to do anything but creep around the bottoms of the canyons, smoldering like a slumbering dragon. Only deep, wet snow would completely kill it.

About that time, Shaman and his family came walking out of the forest. Bolder trotted proudly in front, his coat glowing like a gold coin in the sunlight.

Chapter 22

Storm Cloud

W EEKS LATER, THE ROAD REOPENED INTO THE horse range and I went up Tillet Ridge Road, wondering what I'd find. I was worried about all the horses, especially Sitka. Her condition before the fire was troubling. I was sure she would have tried to foal by now, and I hoped she had survived the experience.

From the open meadows of Tillet, I had a clear view of the mountainside above Crooked Creek Canyon. The checkerboard of burned and unburned forest looked bizarre. Totally burned sections of forest abutted green ones; the blackened hillside gave way again to green trees. Woven into this schizophrenic pattern was a pale rock outcropping arcing dramatically across the mountainside like the delicate wings of a butterfly.

I drove above the Tillet meadows and into the forest. Stumps were all that remained of the hundreds of trees cut by the

 *An older mare had died within a few yards of water.*

I knew a bear had been feeding on the carcass.

firefighters to make a firebreak. Thankfully, the fire never reached here. As I broke out of the limber pines, the Bighorn Mountains dominated the eastern horizon while the dry meadows of the Arrowheads unfolded below. The empty teacup bowl looked parched. So did the open meadows leading to Penn's Cabin. There was not a horse in sight and it was eerily quiet.

Then behind a grove of trees nearly to Penn's, I caught a glimpse of horses. They were clipping the last blades of green grass around the edges of the trees. I hiked toward them and found Red Raven, Blue Sioux, and their foal. The mare and stallion groomed each other, while their sturdy baby looked on. At just three months old, he was so plump that his round little butt had a dimple in the middle.

I hiked on and found horses secreted away in the forested glens. The flick of an ear or the swish of a tail was all that revealed their presence to me. A few yards farther down, I nearly stepped on a blue grouse, who flushed into a nearby fir. The heavy bird thrashed around, trying to find a limb strong enough to support his weight. I could hear the branches breaking and then it was quiet except for the ruffling of his wings. I didn't know which one of us was more startled.

The little path that wandered through the forest ended at the spring-fed water hole. There were no horses around, but tracks confirmed they'd been there. As I skirted the water hole's edge, the stench of death hit me like a slap in the face. *Oh, no,* I thought. *Sitka?* I looked around and didn't see anything immediately. Then directly across the water I spotted dark legs sticking up above the bank. It was a dead horse. As I got closer, I saw it was not a blue roan but a dun. She was an older mare who had been thin in spring and hadn't gained weight over the summer. She had died within a few yards of water. I knew a bear had been feeding on the carcass for the mare's frame had been twisted into an unnatural shape. In the soft mud on the edge of the water hole, I found the round front paw print of a bear—fresh and large. *Probably not the little crippled bear*, I concluded. *More likely a big male.*

About that time, Shaman and his family came walking out of the forest. Bolder trotted proudly in front, his coat glowing like a gold coin in the sunlight. Splash followed him and in unison the two broke into a run for water. Bolder nipped at the foal and she dashed ahead of him. The two were quite close, even though they were a year apart in age.

As the mares neared the water, I saw a newborn foal clinging to the side of her *grulla* mother, Cedar. This lovely young Raven daughter had foaled, and the *grulla* filly at her side was tiny and feminine. A narrow blaze ran down her face, dipped over one nostril, and was punctuated with that characteristic pink snip on the tip of the nose. When she yawned, I could see the toothless pink gums of a very new baby. It can take up to a week for the first teeth to break through the gums. The filly had a dorsal stripe like her mother's, leg stripes, and even delicate dark shoulder stripes. What a beautiful, primitive-looking little foal. She must surely echo back to a time when all horses were camouflaged to survive against giant predators such as dire wolves and American lions, who dwarfed saber-toothed cats and hunted, at least part of the time, in packs.

When she yawned, I could see the toothless pink gums of a very new baby.

The remains of an American lion had been found in caves just across the canyon in the Bighorn Mountains.

The band splashed into the water with the new foal wading right in. *So unafraid*, I thought. Bolder churned up the water, then stopped. The entire band looked toward the forest. The mares spun out of the water, nearly knocking over the tiny foal. When they swung around, their eyes were riveted on the trees. I focused my binoculars on openings in the forest and saw the source of the excitement. A dark red shape—the cinnamon bear—lumbered away through the trees. How close was he when I was looking at his track? In seconds, he was gone.

Bolder moved closer to Shaman and playfully took hold of his stepfather's mane. Shaman was quick to discipline the colt, laying his ears back menacingly. I wondered what Shaman would do with Bolder next spring when the first of his mares foaled. I imagined Bolder would be curious, perhaps, even amorous. To avoid inbreeding, the band stallions usually expel their sons around their second birthday or when one of the mares comes in heat. I guessed that Shaman would boot him out, and Bolder would become a footloose bachelor. I could just imagine him racing around the Arrowheads, his flaxen mane and tail flying.

Red Raven, Blue Sioux, and their foal arrived, and both bands shared the pond together. Their foal saw Bolder and marched up to the big palomino and took hold of his neck. They started to play almost like equals rather than yearling and foal. I saw Cloud do this once as a foal, but I hadn't seen it since. These two Raven grandsons danced around, biting each other's legs and necks. The foal reared up and put his legs around Bolder's neck. As Bolder moved forward, the colt toppled into a heap on the ground only to bounce back up. Out of the corner of my eye I saw Red Raven coming toward Bolder, who began to open and close his mouth

The foal saw Bolder and marched up to the big palomino and took hold of his neck.

This was no fragile newborn, but a strong, sturdy male. He was two weeks old at least.

rapidly and bend his knees to make himself smaller. The teeth clacking and submissive posture meant one thing: *Don't hurt me, I'm little.*

Bolder slunk away a few yards then straightened up and walked off as if nothing had happened. He caught up with Shaman's band and bumped up against the sorrel filly, Splash. She reacted by prancing playfully around Bolder and following him up the trail. All the horses I'd seen looked well. I didn't detect any wheezing or coughing from smoke inhalation. But the big question remained. Where were Sitka and Cloud?

I hiked toward the Crow vision quests on high ground, where I could survey wide expanses of meadows. I was rewarded with a brief glimpse of Cloud, but my heart sank. He walked behind a grove of trees by himself. *Alone, surely he isn't really alone*, I worried. I headed after him. Within ten minutes, I was standing where I had seen him. Looking around, I saw nothing. Behind me, Shaman and his band were coming in my direction. I kept walking and saw Cloud again. He darted through the trees at a gallop, and I lost him again. I stopped and listened. It was quiet. Then I heard a branch break and the little noise of horses blowing air out their noses. I followed the sound. As I came into a sunny opening within a cluster of firs, I breathed a deep sigh.

Cloud was not alone. He was with his family, and they were all there—plus one more. A little dark foal with a big star was nibbling on Cloud's mane. The stallion ignored the baby and started to graze. This was no fragile newborn, but a strong, sturdy male. He was two weeks old at least. I moved and the colt saw me. I stopped immediately and waved. He stared at me then glanced at his mother, who looked up briefly while grazing. No one else in his family seemed upset, so the colt decided he wouldn't be either. He walked in front of his mother, stopping her forward motion. *Let me nurse*, he was saying. She stood still and as he suckled, I moved slowly around to get a better view of Sitka's right side. The bulge in

Everyone in the family moved obediently.
All but one, that is. The foal stood his
ground, staring defiantly at his father.

her flank was still there, as big as ever. It hadn't been the colt lying sideways after all. What was it then? A hernia? An abscess? A tumor? I knew Sitka was still in danger, and I worried about her and the colt. If she were to die in the coming months, so would the colt. But the mare acted as though she felt fine.

Shaman's band had moved into the glen and was perhaps only one hundred feet or so from Cloud's family. Cloud only looked up and then went back to eating. This was normal for two band stallions who knew and respected each other. Bolder went to Flint and grabbed the back of his neck. Flint wheeled and kicked at him. That didn't stop the palomino. He reached down and nipped at Flint's back legs. Flint responded with a well-aimed kick that landed squarely on Bolder's chest. If he felt anything, Bolder didn't let on. He just kept trying to get Flint to really play. *What a beautiful pair of yearlings*, I thought. Flint was finally sleek, his coat of steel-gray shiny. He was smaller than Bolder. Only time would tell if his size and any residual problems with his leg would prevent him from becoming a band stallion. It was quite possible that the two would become bachelor stallions together in the spring.

Over the next few days, I watched Cloud, his little son, and the rest of the band. Temperatures cooled and the horses drifted back out into the open meadows. Cloud's old nemesis, Mateo, was quite close to Sitka, so Cloud snaked the band away from him. Everyone in the family moved obediently. All but one, that is. The foal stood his ground, staring defiantly at his father. Cloud did not hesitate to act. He laid his ears flat and rushed at the colt, reaching out with his teeth bared. The colt dashed forward, out of reach. Instead of teeth clacking, however, he ran and bucked as if playing a game. He circled and spun and bucked some more before joining in lockstep with his mother as if he were the most well behaved colt on the Arrowhead Mountains.

Under the warm sun, Flint lay
down and Storm lay next to him,
their bodies gently touching.

Cloud arched his neck and lifted his head
into the wind, looking for all the world
like the King of the Mountain.

196

Oh, my, I thought. *You have your work cut out for you with this one, Cloud*. I was reminded of a colt seven years ago, who also acted as if the world revolved around him—a sturdy white colt with an attitude. Now the colt I was watching was dark, but in spirit he was much the same. "Storm Cloud," I whispered. I named Cloud's son Storm.

The family moved to the edge of a high hill from which the entire range was in view: Sykes and Tillet, the desert below, and the Bighorn Mountains to the east. Under the warm sun, Flint lay down and Storm lay next to him, their bodies gently touching. Then they went to sleep. *Brothers and good friends*, I thought. Sitka, her daughter, and Sand grazed nearby, while Cloud walked to the summit and stood perfectly still.

A gust of wind lifted Cloud's forelock off his chiseled head. His white mane and tail floated on the breeze. He glanced back at his family, then turned and stared out over his wilderness kingdom. I sensed that greatness was just around the corner for the stallion I had followed, worried over, and admired from the time he was a tottering newborn. As if he could read my mind, Cloud arched his neck and lifted his head into the wind, looking for all the world like the King of the Mountain.

WILD HORSE ORGANIZATIONS

The following organizations are interested in wild horse preservation.
Combined, they represent over 8,000,000 Americans.

American Horse Defense Fund
11206 Valley View Drive
Kensington, MD 20895
(866) 983-3456 (toll free)
www.ahdf.org
ahdforg@aol.com

American Mustang and Burro Association
P.O. Box 788
Lincoln, CA 95648
(530) 633-9271
www.bardalisa.com/bardalisa/
AMBAInc@bardalisa.com

American Society for the Prevention of Cruelty to Animals (ASPCA)
Federal Legislative Office
1755 Massachusetts Avenue NW, Suite 418
Washington, D.C. 20036
(202) 232-5020
www.aspca.org

Animal Legal Defense Fund
401 East Jefferson, Suite 206
Rockville, MD 20850
(301) 294-1617
www.aldf.org

Animal Protection Institute
P.O. Box 22505
Sacramento, CA 95822
(916) 731-5521
www.api4animals.org

Animal Welfare Institute
P.O. Box 3650
Washington, D.C. 20007
(703) 836-4300
www.awionline.org

Colorado Wild Horse and Burro Coalition
2406 Fifteenth Avenue Court
Greeley, CO 80631
(970) 356-8509
bflores@lamar.colostate.edu

Doris Day Animal League
227 Massachusetts Avenue, NE Suite 100
Washington, D.C. 20002
(202) 546-1761
www.ddal.org

DreamCatcher Wild Horse and Burro Sanctuary
P.O. Box 6497
Lancaster, CA 93539
831-818-7421

Front Range Equine Rescue
P.O. Box 38068
Colorado Springs, CO 80937-8068
(719)-495-6389
www.frontrangeequinerescue.org

The Fund for Animals
8121 Georgia Avenue, Suite 301
Silver Spring, MD 20910
(301)-585-2591
www.fund.org

Hooved Animal Humane Society
10804 McConnell Road
Woodstock, IL 60098
(815) 337-5563
www.hahs.org

Hooved Animal Rescue and Protection Society
312 East Main Street
Barrington, IL 60010-0094
(847) 382-0503
www.harpsonline.org
info@harpsonline.org

Humane Society of the United States
700 Professional Drive
Gaithersburg, MD 20879
(202) 452-1100
www.hsus.org

International Society for the Protection of Mustangs and Burros
HCR 53 Box 7C
Interior, SD 57750
(605) 433-5600

Return to Freedom
American Wild Horse Sanctuary
P.O. Box 926
Lompoc, CA 93436
(805)735-3246
www.returntofreedom.org
neda@returntofreedom.org

Wild Horse Spirit
25 Lewers Creek Road
Carson City, NV 89704
(775) 883-5488
www.wildhorsespirit.org
wildhorses@pyramid.net

Selected Bibliography

Ainslie, Tom, and Bonnie Ledbetter. *The Body Language of Horses.* New York: William Morrow and Company, Inc., 1980.

Berger, Joel. *Wild Horses of the Great Basin: Social Competition and Population Size.* Chicago: The University of Chicago Press, 1986.

Clutton-Brock, Juliet. *Horse Power: A History of the Horse and the Donkey in Human Societies.* Cambridge, Massachusetts: Harvard University Press, 1992.

Curtin, Sharon. *Mustang: Our Horses, Our Land.* Bearsville, New York: Rufus Publications, Inc., 1996.

Dobie, J. Frank. *The Mustangs.* New York: Bramhall House, 1952.

Donahue, Debra L. *The Western Range Revisited: Removing Livestock from Public Lands to Conserve Native Biodiversity.* Norman, Oklahoma: University of Oklahoma Press, 1999.

Dossenbach, Monique, and D. Hans. *The Noble Horse.* Auckland, New Zealand: David Bateman Ltd., 1997.

Edwards, Elwyn Hartley. *Wild Horses: A Spirit Unbroken.* Vancouver, British Columbia: Voyageur Press, Inc., 1995.

Kirkpatrick, Jay F. *Into the Wind: Wild Horses of North America.* Minocqua, Wisconsin: NorthWord Press, 1994.

McDonnell, Sue. *The Equid Ethogram: A Practical Field Guide to Horse Behavior.* Lexington, Kentucky: Eclipse Press, 2003.

MacFadden, Bruce J. *Fossil Horses: Systematics, Paleobiology, and Evolution of the Family Equidae.* New York: Cambridge University Press, 1992.

McBane, Susan, and Helen Douglas-Cooper. *Horse Facts.* New York: Barnes and Noble Books, 1991.

Parelli, Pat, with Kathy Kadash. *Natural Horse-Man-Ship.* Colorado Springs, Colorado: Western Horseman, 1993.

Ryden, Hope. *America's Last Wild Horses.* New York: The Lyons Press, 1999.

Scanlan, Lawrence. *Wild About Horses: Our Timeless Passion for the Horse.* New York: Harper Collins, 1998.

Sponenberg, D. Philip, and Bonnie V. Beaver. *Horse Color: A Complete Guide to Horse Coat Colors.* Ossining, New York: Breakthrough Publications, 1983.

Cast of Characters

Blackie: former band stallion; one of the older horses on the range; solid black

Black Mare: the mother of Little Cloud; a member of Shaman's Band; originally with Plenty Coups

Blue Sioux: Red Raven's mare; a blue roan who was originally with Plenty Coups

Bolder: Little Cloud's name when he approached one year old

Cascade: black-brown filly daughter of Electra and Mateo named for the waterfall blaze on her face

Cedar: solid *grulla* mare; daughter of Raven and Grumpy Grulla; Cloud's half sister

Challenger: *grulla* stallion killed by lightning in 1999

Chino: buckskin band stallion

Cloud: pale palomino band stallion; son of Raven and the palomino mare; half brother of Diamond, Red Raven, Cedar, and Electra

Cloud's filly: foal born to Queen and sired by Cloud

Diamond: Cloud's half brother; son of Raven and the claybank buckskin mare; blue roan

Electra: Cloud's half sister; daughter of Raven and the claybank buckskin Mare; red roan with a lightning bolt mark on her face; in Mateo's band

Flint: *grulla* son of Sitka and Shaman, but raised from birth by Cloud

Grumpy Grulla: Raven's stern lead mare; solid *grulla*

King: old former band stallion; mahogany bay

Konik: former band stallion who dies; *grulla*

Little Cloud: pale palomino son of Cloud and Black Mare; born in Shaman's band; later named Bolder

Mateo: dark bay band stallion. As a four-year-old, Cloud tried to steal Mateo's band

Morning Star: dark bay band stallion with a star

PK aka Preacher's Kid: son of The Rev; yearling playmate of Bolder

Plenty Coups: blue roan band stallion; Cloud tried to steal Plenty Coups's band in 2000; named for the great Crow Chief Plenty Coups

Queen: Cloud's first mare; solid *grulla* mother of the Red Dun Yearling and Cloud's filly

Raven: Cloud's father; black stallion with a star and snip and long forelock; the most dominant stallion on the Arrowheads until recently; most successful producer of reproducing mares and stallions on the Arrowheads

Red Dun Yearling: blaze-faced son of Queen and King

Red Raven: son of Raven and the claybank buckskin mare; Cloud's half brother; red roan with broken blaze; one year younger than Cloud

Sand: Blue Sioux and Red Raven's daughter; sandy colored roan

Shaman: dun band stallion; longtime band stallion on the Arrowheads; stepfather of Bolder

Sitka: the blue roan mare in Cloud's band; formerly a mare in Shaman's band; mother of Flint

Splash: filly daughter of Shaman and a dun mare; one year younger than Bolder; sorrel with broken blaze

Star: bay band stallion with a star

Starbuck: dun band stallion; lives in red desert and lower Sykes Ridge year round

Storm Cloud: son of Cloud and Sitka; dark colt with large star; Color will probably be blue or brown roan

the palomino: Cloud's mother; pale palomino but darker than Cloud; in Diamond's band

The Rev: red roan band stallion; father of PK

Trace: Ginger's blue roan wild horse bought at BLM auction in 1997 as a yearling; full name is Absarokee Trace.

Horse Markings

blaze: white stripe on face that runs from between the eyes to the nose

blue roan: black and white body hair mixed together; black head, mane, tail, and legs

bay: shades of reddish brown with black points, black mane and tail

bay roan: reddish brown and white body hair mixed together; brown head, mane, tail, and legs

buckskin: yellow or tan body with black points

claybank buckskin: pale buckskin; color matches the riverbanks near the Arrowheads; sacred color to some Native American tribes

dun: used here for zebra dun with primitive marks over withers; body color tan to dark golden brown with black mane, tail, and legs

grulla: silver gray to slate gray body color with primitive marks of dorsal stripe, leg stripes, and stripe over withers; Spanish word for "sandhill crane–colored"

mahogany bay: dark red bay

palomino: various shades of yellow with light mane and tail

points: edges of the ears, mane, tail, and lower legs; all horses have either black points (duns, *grullas*, bays) or nonblack points (sorrels, red roans, palominos)

primitive marks: dorsal stripe, leg stripes, and shoulder stripes

red roan: red and white body hairs; red head, mane, and tail

roan: white and a color mixed on the body; head, mane, and tail are the nonwhite color

snip: a white or pink mark between a horse's nostrils, extending into or near the nostrils

sorrel: red body; red to near white (flaxen) mane and tail

star: white mark on forehead